Sharing the Maskmaking Journey

Sharing the Maskmaking Journey

A *Faces of Your Soul* Teacher's Manual

Elise Dirlam Ching and Kaleo Ching

KALEONAHE PRESS

Walnut Creek, California

KALEONAHE PRESS
Walnut Creek, California

www.kaleoching.com

Most photos by Kaleo Ching
Cover photo and photo of Charon by Lee Fatheree
Other photos by John Pearson, Annalisa Adelberg,
and Lyn 'Unihipiliowailelepualu Hilliard

Cover and text design by Lyn 'Unihipiliowailelepualu Hilliard

Some of the material in this manual contains excerpts and photos from the books by Elise and Kaleo Ching, *Faces of Your Soul: Rituals in Art, Maskmaking, and Guided Imagery with Ancestors, Spirit Guides, and Totem Animals,* published by North Atlantic Books, copyright © 2006, and *Chi and Creativity: Vital Energy and Your Inner Artist,* published by Blue Snake Books, copyright © 2007.

Disclaimer: The information contained in this book is intended to supplement, not substitute for, the above mentioned book, *Faces of Your Soul,* as well as the user's own wisdom and experience. It does not substitute for educational, art, or counseling training or legal advice. Suggestions offered are based on the authors' personal experience and should be adjusted to the individual knowledge and experience of the user of this manual.

ISBN 978-0615437989

Mahalo ke akua mau loa

In gratitude to the divine

Contents

Introduction

By now you have obtained and read our (Kaleo and Elise's) experiential book, *Faces of Your Soul: Rituals in Art, Maskmaking, and Guided Imagery with Ancestors, Spirit Guides, and Totem Animals* (North Atlantic Books, 2006), to which references in this manual refer. You have made masks, hopefully several of them, and feel comfortable with the techniques. You have journeyed into the depths of your subconscious, experimented with your favorite forms of art and journaling, and shared your discoveries with others. You have experienced joy and transformation, and now you want to share this journey with others.

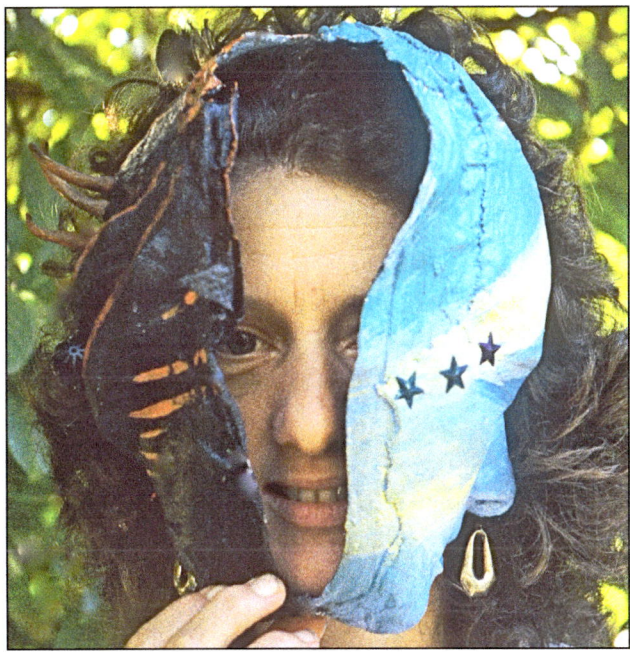

Orion's Child

Whether you are an art teacher, a psychotherapist leading groups in expressive arts healing journeys, a leader of collaborative body/mind/spirit retreats, a corporate facilitator for employee well-being, or any of a multitude of other roles guiding others in transformative process, we are delighted that you want to incorporate work of unmasking faces of the soul.

In the hundreds of classes and workshops we have taught and for the thousands of students we have encountered, we have found the maskmaking journey to add a powerful dimension to many forms of inner exploration. The mask is much more than a mirror of the persona. It is a mirror of the soul. Let this Teacher's Manual support you in this endeavor of teaching and sharing maskmaking. It is our hope that our own experience in this work will guide you to share this transformative journey with your own communities.

Philosophy of Teaching

We approach the teaching of creative process as an experiment. There are some essential guidelines in the areas of safety and respect of others, time, space, process, and materials. But in the areas of creative techniques and course content requirement, we emphasize permission and freedom over rules. An atmosphere of support and encouragement is essential for the subconscious to feel safe to let its treasures rise to the surface and flow forward in creativity. We prefer to keep the vessel of the classroom open and to focus on making suggestions that open doors so the students make their own discoveries, see creative options, and then make their own choices.

We emphasize that the class is a crucible in which magic happens. And each of us, whether teacher or student, maskmaker or maskgiver, speaker or listener, plays an integral role in making that magic happen. And, in fact, roles interact and interweave, and we are all transformed, not only from our own creative journeys, but from the sacred work of sharing them with others.

The Student-Teacher Relationship

We like to integrate the body, spirit, and mind (subconscious and conscious) through the ancient rituals of Chi Kung movement, guided imagery/hypnosis, and art. Chi Kung movement, based on Traditional Chinese Medicine, engages the body, chakras, organ-meridians, and deep extraordinary vessels. On a high level, Chi Kung engages the subconscious. Through Chi Kung one can enter into the spaciousness where spiritual connections can be made. Guided imagery leads deeper into subconscious realms where inner guides, landscapes, treasures, and wisdom await. Art gives visual and tactile form to the discoveries and bridges the inner and the outer realms.

Taoists, shamans, traditional healers, mystics, and artists have long used forms of hypnosis, trance, music, movement, guided imagery, and art as ways of channeling and accessing the subconscious realms and alternative realities. Seekers on the journey of life face many choices. Everyone is capable of healing or wounding, growing or deteriorating, creating or destroying, and the imagination as well can be used to create or destroy. Accessing the depths of the psyche can be scary, but what an adventure! Chi Kung, guided imagery, and art are, for us, alternative medicine, ritual, ceremony, and processes for deepening insight and healing the body spiritually, physically, mentally, emotionally, and energetically. When the teacher, guiding others with clear intention and mindful compassion, shares these processes, they can be vehicles to support the path of movement toward one's highest potential, one's highest Self.

How to integrate these forms of healing in modern life? Through the experience of cleansing and purification, understanding and clarity, joy and contentment, self-empowerment and compassion for others, that these modalities offer.

For you as teachers, we urge you to teach from the integration of your soul, mind, heart, and body. Express from your soul, focus with your mind, expand with your heart, create with your body. Then inspire others to feel their bodies and emotions; to want to deepen their understanding of their souls; to give themselves permission to take risks and empower themselves through creativity; to seek comfort and guidance in the spiritual realm. Inspire your students to move with a sense of exploration, to dive in with a sense of discovery, and to create with freedom, awe, and joy. Inspire your students to trust their deepest selves and to reach for their highest Selves.

Embrace your students with the structure of your class, its space, its timing, its plan. Nurture them with abundance. Inspire them with enthusiasm. Encourage them to push the margins of awareness while you care for them with patience and timing. At the same time take care of yourself as teacher through knowing your boundaries and respecting your own time, space, and privacy, just as you respect those of others. This is the fine art of Yang and Yin balance applied to the soul work of teaching—practicing abundance with boundaries.

In sharing with others, we find it very helpful to imagine that we become the students watching us, the teachers, as they ready their psyches for the journey of creative self-exploration. This helps us to understand how to teach the class. We also understand that there are many doors and many ways of entering each doorway.

Most students ask: How is this process pertinent for me? How does this help me in my daily life? In my career? In my spiritual life?

An artist might ask: How will this help me to learn more about who I am as an artist, my motivation, my art techniques, my creative growth? When I graduate with an art degree, how is this going to help me find a job? Can it help me deepen my relationship with my muse?

A teenager might ask: Is this more parental bullshit? Will this help me answer who I am and what I want? Will it be about what really matters to me?

An inmate in prison might ask: Is this a trap? Someone trying to analyze me? Categorize me? Trick me into revealing my secrets? How will it help me face life behind bars?

For a teacher/group leader: What can this teach me about bringing more harmony, cooperation, fun, and understanding within the group? What can it show me about the best of myself that I have to share with others?

For a shaman: How can this take me deeper into the lower world? How can it integrate the dark soul with the light? How can it deepen my relationship with my totem animal and the natural world? How can I incorporate maskmaking in my work to deepen the connections with my apprentices, create ritual and ceremony, and access the realms of my ancestors and guides through archetypes, forms, textures, and colors?

For a person in emotional crisis or distress: How can I get relief from my pain and anxiety? How will this ground and center me? How will it help me find hope, joy, and strength? Will this help provide clarity and belief in myself? Will this open the doors to my spiritual helpers and guides?

For a psychotherapist: How can I use this process to help me understand and support my clients? How can I use it with clients to encourage them on their paths of self-understanding and empowerment?

For a spiritual seeker: How can this creative journey make me more aware of and deepen my relationship with the Divine? With my guardian angels? With my spirit guides?

For a bodyworker: How can I use this to gain more insight and deepen my wisdom? Will it help me become more sensitive and deepen the work I do with clients? Will it help me to access subconscious levels, enhance my relationship with the Creator, and make my bodywork more spiritual? Will it inspire me to treat the body as a living sculpture or canvas?

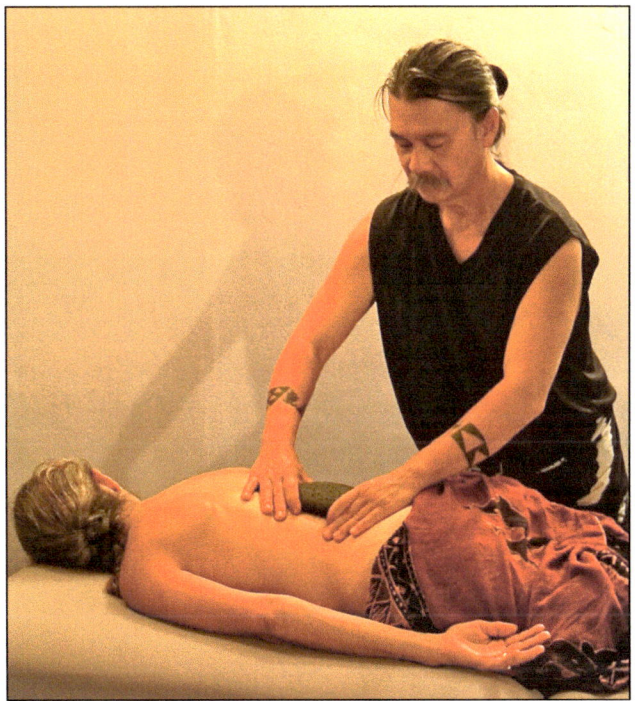

Bodywork and hypnotherapy: portals to creativity

For a hypnotherapist: How can Chi Kung movement, guided imagery, and art help me to explore the subconscious and bridge the inner wisdom and creativity for my work with clients? How is art a form of induction and ideomotor response?

Whatever life paths your students follow, each individual is unique, and each group has its own collective personality. What works effectively with one person or group may not work as well with another. Accept these differences with appreciation and with awareness that this process can be transformative for anyone, no matter what background and issues come to the maskmaking table. For the table is an altar for honoring the creativity, self-expression, and the Divine presence in each person. What matters is not the creative object but the work and play, the exploration and discovery, the self-understanding and self-sharing in the realm of the muse. We tell our students it is not the art object, but the process of making it, which is sacred.

Preparing the Body and Soul

We have found that it is helpful to combine creative work with some sort of meditative movement to awaken, balance, and engage the body. The subconscious is more receptive if the body is open and relaxed, free of tensions, with energy flowing smoothly. We often use Chi Kung, as it is a core practice we both share, and it is especially effective for gently but powerfully engaging one's being on all levels, physical, energetic, emotional, mental, and spiritual.

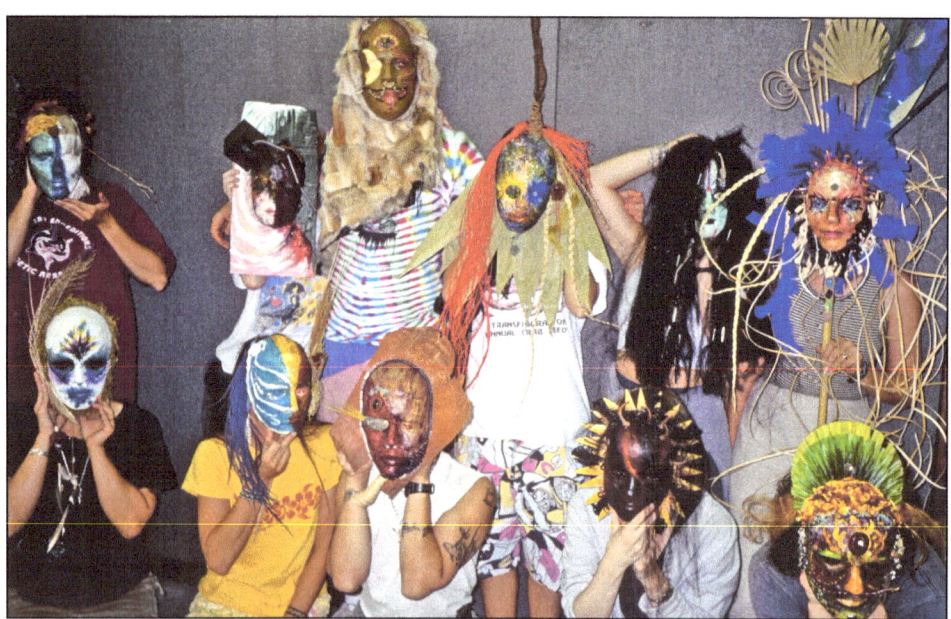

Integrating Tai Chi and Maskmaking (with Jarl Forsman, Kaleo, and Elise)

More specifically, Chi Kung engages and balances the chakras, centers of energy, intelligence, emotions, and spirit along the Microcosmic Orbit. The Macrocosmic Orbit helps to ground, focus, and center (earth) and to foster awareness that life's work is transcendent (work of the soul/heaven). The

SHARING THE MASKMAKING JOURNEY

chakras are ways to receive information and expand energies to touch someone in a deeper way. For more on our principles and practices with Chi Kung, including the Micro- and Macrocosmic Orbits and chakras, see our book *Chi and Creativity: Vital Energy and Your Inner Artist* (Blue Snake Books, 2007).

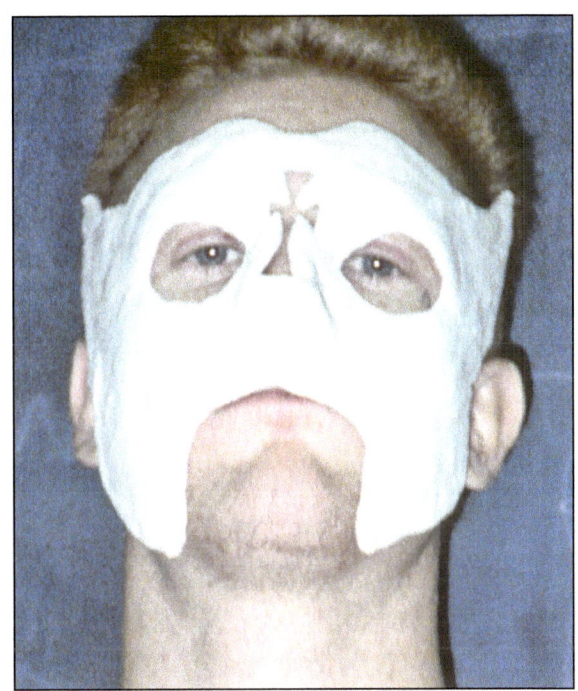

Maskmaking in the Jail Psychiatric Unit

When Kaleo taught Chi Kung, guided imagery, and maskmaking in the San Francisco County Jail Psychiatric Unit, he worked with maximum and minimum security inmates. In the mornings he did Tiger's Breath Chi Kung to ground, engage the chakras, and build his Chi (this enlarges, whereas fear contracts). Making his Chi and its vibrations large and full of positive caring and support helped to create sacred space within this classroom behind steel and shatter-proof glass.

In class, he used other Chi vibrations (voice/throat chakra) to calm, support, and engage the inmates in creative process. He used intuition (third eye) to work with them in an intuitive way. He used caring and joy (heart chakra) to fill the room with positive energy.

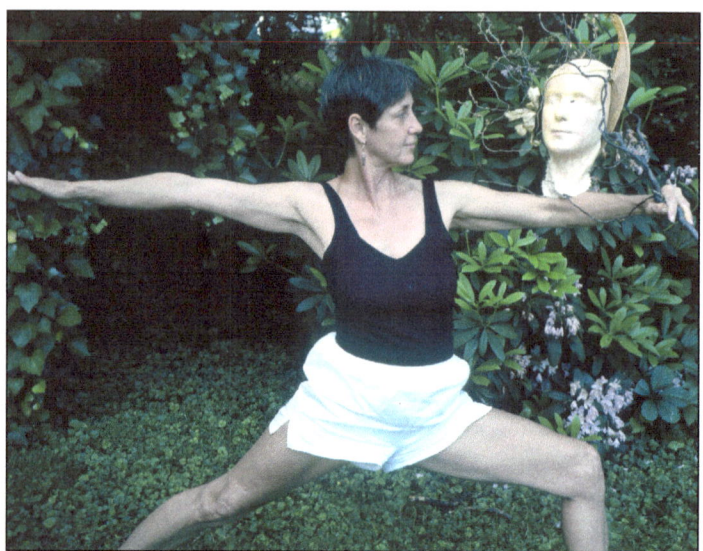

Integrating Yoga and Maskmaking (with Rodney Yee, Kaleo, and Elise)

To prepare the body as a vessel of creativity and soul-work, we have also found hatha yoga to be an effective complement, as well as Tai Chi, experimental dance, hula, and bodywork. The possibilities are numerous. You may have your own practice to bring to the process, or you may collaborate with a co-teacher, where you lead the maskmaking and the other leads the meditative movement.

Guided Journeying

This is not a comprehensive manual in how to lead guided imagery journeys, but simply a few words of encouragement to share your gifts with others and to complement what you know and do. If you are a teacher of art or yoga, a group facilitator or a psychotherapist, a parent or a trusted confidante, you have probably had experience guiding people into inner awareness. You may have read your children a comforting bedtime story, using your voice and embellishing with your own words to lull them into pleasing dreams. You may have guided your yoga students hundreds of times in savasana ("corpse pose," restorative lying meditation) at the end of asana (posture) practice. As a psychotherapist, you may have guided a client experiencing emotional distress to breathe deeply, to feel the emotions in her body, to connect with areas of holding or blockage and explore them for greater understanding and integration.

You may already have your own style and techniques for guided journeys. You may use other modalities and supports as guides into the inner realms. Perhaps you are practiced in shamanic drumming. Or you can support your gentle guidance with meditative music. If you sing, you may want to lead the group in and out with a chant or soft song. Stay with what you are comfortable using and build on it. Please feel free to use the guided imagery processes in our books, Faces of Your Soul and Chi and Creativity. Modify them to your personality and also to the experience and needs of your students or clients.

Whether or not you are experienced guiding inner journeys, lean toward the side of simplicity. It is preferable to leave the subconscious ready for more rather than to overwhelm it.

Induction—the journey down into the realms of the subconscious—is very important to relax the students/clients (in our classes, we often use the breath as a vehicle for induction). Induction readies the fertile ground of the subconscious. The subconscious yields best when it feels nurtured. Start with simple relaxation techniques and breath awareness. If you have not done this before, try it on yourself, especially when you are doing your own sitting or moving meditation practice. Use body awareness as a beginning and ending and the breath as a way in and a way out of the guided journey. Try to feel the Chi (energy) of the students. If it is Yang (excessive and high), then you might want to lower the vibrations with your voice and speak into their Tan Tiens (haras). If their vibrational Chi is Yin (sleepy and watery), you can talk into their third eye chakras to pick up their energy. Normally, when we lead students in a group guided imagery, we speak to their heart chakras to induce calm and comfort and to encourage accessing their inner wisdom and hearts' desires. Your voice is the means of connection between your intention as guide and the subconscious awareness of each participant. So use your voice as if it were a musical instrument tuned to lull the listeners into subconscious realms.

The suggestions herein build on the "Guidelines for Guided Imagery" for self-practice in Faces of Your Soul (pp. xxv-xxvi), summarized as follows:

• To practice guided imagery, be in a comfortable meditative position.

• Let the guided journey be a path inviting exploration beyond, according to your own inner wisdom.

- Let each journey take you deeper.

- Notice the interweaving of the journeys with each other and with your daily life.

- Set your intention before you begin; then let it recede to the back of your awareness.

- Start from a serene and safe place in your inner world, to which you may return at any time.

- Make sure your inner guides have your best interests at heart.

- Let your breath help guide you.

- Realize the inner journey may have challenges that your subconscious feels you are ready to engage.

- When the journey ends, channel inner challenges and discoveries in art, writing, and/or movement.

- Keep in touch with your guides in daily life.

We want to emphasize the safe place and the supportive nature of inner guides (see *Faces of Your Soul* pp. 9-14). When we lead journeys from this foundation, we have found, in our twenty years of leading guided imagery, that almost all journey experiences are either positive and inspiring or else challenging in ways the journeyers feel ready to experience. A serene and safe place is a refuge the journeyer can return to at any time if some exploration into subconscious realms becomes disturbing. We strengthen the safety of this place by inviting each journeyer to find a circle of empowerment and protection—a circle so personal that no one or no thing can enter without the journeyer's permission. And when meeting a new guide, the journeyer asks if it has his or her best interests at heart and, if not, sends it away and asks for the true guide to come forward. Then, at some time in the future, if a guide is no longer helpful or supportive, the journeyer can ask for a new one to appear.

Brainwaves and Guided Imagery Journeys

Brainwaves are electrical impulses that reflect levels of brain activity and can be recorded by electroencephalography (EEG). Brainwaves are measured in Hertz, or cycles per second, with the fastest waves (beta) having the lowest amplitudes and the slowest waves (delta) having the highest amplitudes. Brainwave patterns change when you enter the realms of the subconscious through guided imagery. There are four main patterns in the living human brain that reveal levels of alertness from hyper-vigilance to deepest dreamless sleep.

The range of Hertz for each type varies according to source, so the ranges following are approximate:

- Beta (≈14-30 Hz): alert, waking consciousness, with >30 escalating to the stress (fight-or-flight) response, high anxiety, and panic

- Alpha (≈8-13 Hz): relaxation, day-dreaming, light trance, light meditation, self-hypnosis, creative imagination, beginning access to subconscious messages and enhanced receptivity to learning

- Theta (≈4-7 Hz): dream phase (REM) sleep, trance, deep hypnosis, deep meditation, greater access to subconscious messages, creative breakthroughs, and positive learning

- Delta (≈1-3 Hz): dreamless sleep, deep trance with loss of body awareness, access to archetypal images from the collective unconscious

- Death (0 Hz): amplitude zero, no measurable brain activity

Brainwave patterns give you a mental picture for identifying levels of consciousness. Different patterns originate in different parts of the brain. Thus, mental activity is an interactive matrix. It shifts from moment to moment, depending on external and internal stimuli.

How this awareness influences you as guide for the inner journey is to offer insight into how the environment of the journey space—including your words and style, the mood you create, the ambience of the room, and the rapport among group members—interacts with the mind of each voyager, even as the mind of the voyager is responding to its own inner processes.

A hypothetical rendition of a well-known story from 19th century science illustrates the potential of the dialogue between the conscious and the subconscious mind via the interaction of brainwave states. Imagine chemist Friedrich August Kekule, after many years studying carbon bonding (beta state activity), sitting down in an easy chair at the end of a long day of work and lapsing into a day-dream (alpha) of carbon atoms dancing before his mind's eye. As he sinks deeper into relaxation, he loses touch with his surroundings and falls into a dreamless trancelike sleep (delta). Then a far-off ringing of a bell rouses him slightly (theta), and a vision appears—the archetypal ouroboros, a snake with its tail in its mouth forming a hoop. When he surfaces to a dreamy awakening (alpha), the answer to the riddle that has been puzzling him for years is clear. The shape of the benzene molecule is a ring! Eureka (beta)! He sits up and draws the fresh, clear image from his mind onto paper.

When Kaleo prepares to do art, his alert (beta) awareness readies his art media and guides him in use of techniques. At the same time he hovers at the threshold of alpha, as the familiar colors and textures of the media, the enticing images of his works in progress, and the layers, textures, and rhythms of music invite him to begin to dialogue with the subconscious realms. When he paints, the colors and textures and the movement of his body drop him deeper into a waking-dreamlike alpha state, so that the painting becomes alive with subconscious content. Then sometimes beta mode reasserts itself as he steps back and surveys the landscape of the painting from a distance. His practice of art is an example of the conscious and subconscious in active dialogue.

As you guide your students into relaxation and guided imagery, you invite their own buried treasures from the subconscious to send up clues. You invite the hard work of their lives to reveal submerged truths. But each person comes in a different place of readiness, both in the bigger context of ongoing personal process and the more immediate context of the events of the day.

During any given journey, each voyager will have a unique experience. A man coming in tired from being up all night with a colicky infant may already be drowsy and have a hard time staying in alert beta mode for a lecture but may fall asleep readily in guided imagery and not recall his journey. A woman coming in after a stressful drive on the freeway through rush-hour traffic may be in high beta mode and have a hard time relaxing for guided imagery. She might find her mind resistant to the journey, not because of any fault on her part or the guide's, but because it takes most of the journey time for her to begin to relax. Another woman just coming from reading about the attributes of her totem animal, then sketching its image in her journal, might be perfectly primed and maximally receptive for a journey to subconscious realms.

Through the holistic nature of your class, you have invited the mental, emotional, physical, energetic, and spiritual spheres of the participants into dialogue. Now, as you guide the group from the external demands of coming to class and meeting each other (beta emphasis) into relaxation through meditative movement and your guided imagery induction (alpha) and then deeper into trance (theta), you are inviting the various levels of consciousness to communicate. By keeping in mind the key principles for leading guided imagery below, you can create a context that invites journeyers' minds to enter the relaxed and receptive states of alpha and theta, in which enhanced receptivity to the mysteries and messages of the subconscious mind abides.

Key Principles for Leading Guided Imagery

- Atmosphere is important. Try to have a room that is womb-like—dark, warm, quiet, comfortable. Make sure participants have a comfortable place to sit or lie and pillows and blankets for support and warmth, if possible.

- Practice your journeys on yourself prior to class. Elise loves to do walking Chi Kung in the woods at dawn, then let the quiet trail take her into inner explorations. Kaleo likes to do brief, gentle Chi Kung to engage his inner body, chakras, and meridians then settle into stillness through Zhan Zhuang meditation to travel to the threshold of his inner world.

- The subconscious responds best to simple language. Speak as if to a third or fourth grade child.

- Repetition is fine. The subconscious likes it.

- Use your voice in a gentle, inviting, but confident way to inspire trust and caring.

- Keep your voice low, slow, rhythmic. Use not your speaking voice but your bedtime story voice.

- Allow strategic pauses that give the subconscious time and space to explore.

- Watch and listen to the journeyers' facial expressions, breathing patterns, and body movements for clues. Notice if they are bored, restless, or deep into the trance. Change your voice, your imagery, or your rhythm as appropriate to invite them deeper into the subconscious realms.

- If you encounter noise interference, just let it be and stay confident in your guidance. If a dog is barking or a siren is going by in the distance or a student is coughing or snoring in the room, you can integrate the distraction by saying, "Any sounds you hear just help you to go deeper into relaxation"; or alternatively, "Any sounds outside your inner world seem so very far away."

- Remind the journeyers that their journeys are their own, and even though they are invited to follow your guidance, they should feel free to venture off on their own if desired, trusting in their own inner wisdom, then returning to the guidance of your voice when they are ready. This invitation is important, for the details of a group journey may not always fit for each individual, and offering the subconscious permission to follow its own lead gives it freedom to explore and create.

- Stay in the subconscious realm (trance state). Questions that encourage thinking or analyzing bring the journeyers into the conscious mind.

- Use language that engages all the senses, remembering that some people process more in the visual mode, some in the auditory, some in the kinesthetic, and some in the intuitive, having a subtle interior impression rather than a physical sense of contents and events in the inner world. On the journey, what are the colors and shapes, the sounds, the textures and temperatures? What smells stir buried memories? What tastes arouse emotions? What sixth sense is coming through?

- If your journey includes terrain that is dark, like a cave, a deep forest, or a night landscape, invite journeyers to carry a source of light with them, so that they can see the path and their surroundings.

- Use positive instead of negative images. For example, instead of saying, "Let go of all the worry, anxiety, and frustrations in your body," it is better to say, "Sink deeper into rest, each breath sending a gentle wave of relaxation through your entire body."

- Use open-ended rather than yes/no type questions. Instead of asking, "Would you like to enter the portal?" ask, "How do you enter the portal?" Instead of asking, "Is anyone there to meet you?" ask, "Who is there to meet you?"

- The subconscious often responds to being guided with ample freedom rather than overly rigid structure. Maintain a balance between confident guidance and trusting permissiveness.

- You, as guide, provide a structure and a path to travel on. You are like a friend who has traveled this path before accompanying another with your experience but allowing for freedom of exploration and discovery. You suggest rather than force the direction of the journey.

- Stay on the path. Be careful about asking questions that open doors to terrains too vast to explore in one session.

- Limit each guided imagery session to no more than twenty minutes.

- Always make sure you bring journeyers back to the present time and place.

- Consider how deep the journey was and what happens next on the agenda to determine how much suggestion you need to give participants to return to waking consciousness. If they are to do something requiring alertness after the journey (e.g., driving to lunch, using power tools), bring them all the way back to beta awareness. If they are to do journaling and art immediately after the guided imagery, you may keep them in a more open and relaxed state (alpha) by inviting them to maintain silence and not talk to each other and by keeping the journey music playing. This way, access to the subconscious is more readily available for translation into creativity through words and art.

Journaling

We encourage you and your students to keep journals. How each does this is very personal. We encourage honoring one's own needs and desires for privacy. No one should expect to read another's journal, but there may be parts of a journal one desires to share at certain times. Again, process is of primary importance and freedom is the key (see *Faces of Your Soul* section on Journaling, pp. xxvi-xxvii).

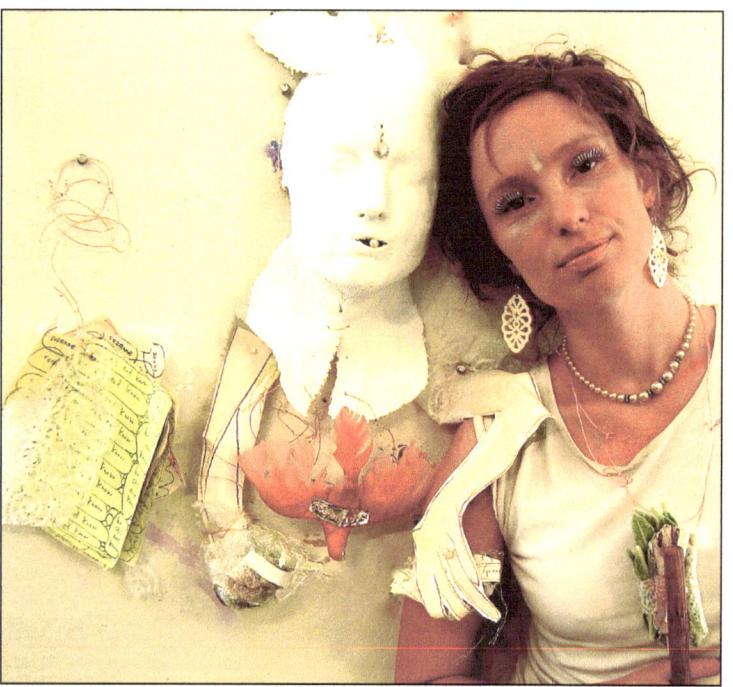

Suzanne: Journal-collage-mask

Art as Process

Art-making is an adventure in creative exploration, yet it has been sullied for many because of experiences of criticism. How often do students say, "I'm not an artist," or, "I can't draw" (or paint or sculpt)? But there is no can't to it. We suggest that students let go of the intention of making a literal illustration of the terrain they experience in the inner world, of the energy they feel in Chi Kung, or of the spirit helpers they encounter on their journeys into the subconscious. Rather, we invite the making of art from the inner terrain, or as the energy body, or through the eyes and hands and being of the spirit guide. Let the art materials entice; let the colors of the paints titillate the muse; let the textures of clay and natural fibers, of furs and feathers, of beads and bones, engage the fingers in the play of the soul (see *Faces of Your Soul* section on Creative Process, pp. xxvii-xxx).

Teachers' Guided Journeys

For the following guided journeys, you may want to read the guided imagery over to yourself until you are familiar with it; or you may have a partner read it to you; or you may record it, then play it back. Then ready yourself for some explorations into the subconscious realms of you, the teacher. Find a space of quiet and a position of comfort where you will not be disturbed.

Your Learning Sanctuary

Intention

In this journey you will travel to your learning sanctuary, a place and time in your life where you felt safe, comfortable, and open to learning.

Guided Imagery

As you inhale and exhale, notice how easily your breath of life flows, naturally in, naturally out. Notice its temperature, its texture, as it comes and goes. Observe how, as each breath becomes longer, slower, and deeper, you naturally sink deeper into relaxation. Savor this moment of gently letting go.

In this comfortable place of rest, your subconscious summons you to a place and time in your life where you find yourself learning something of importance. You feel safe and serene but with a stirring of anticipation and discovery. This is somewhere and sometime in which you felt inspired and secure to inquire, to grow, and to stretch the boundaries of your imagination in a new and positive way.

Where are you? What time of day is it? How old are you? Are you alone or with others? Is there a teacher or guide? What are you learning that makes this experience so alive? Notice the special qualities of the teacher and the situation that help to pique your interest, open your mind, and make you feel emotionally safe.

Take a few moments and feel the excitement of this new territory, the territory around you and the expanding territory you are exploring within you.

What sensations do you feel? How are you changing? Observe and enjoy. When you feel full with this learning experience, return to awareness of your breath coming in, going out, bringing you back to the present time and place.

Journaling

What are your lessons from your journey to your learning sanctuary? What set of circumstances within and around you came together then and there in the past and return to you now in the present journey to make this learning experience profound and effective? What do you find special about this teacher, this situation? What about this experience impacts you as a teacher now?

Your Mentor/Teacher/Guide

Intention

In this journey you will meet and interact with a spiritual guide, a mentor, or a teacher—someone who has profoundly inspired you. You may or may not have met this person face-to-face. You may have read a biography of this person. You may have dreamed about this person. This mentor will be there to accompany you as you move forward in your journey of mentoring others through the sharing of the maskmaking process.

Your mentor may be a famous director, a writer, an artist, an inventor, an explorer. It could be Maya Angelou or Hafiz, Frida Kahlo or Claude Monet, Albert Einstein or Amelia Earhart.

Your mentor could be a spiritual teacher like the Dalai Lama, a shaman 1,000 years ago, or the mysterious figure of Lao Tzu. It could be Christ or Mary Magdalene, Buddha or Kwan Yin, Mohammed or Moses, the Green Tara or Kali.

Your mentor might be a personal advisor, perhaps a high school art teacher who handed you the end of the thread leading to your muse. It might be your own ancestor. Kaleo finds inspiration and guidance from his Korean ancestor, born in the 10th century A.D., Choi Ch'ung. Kaleo includes Ch'ung's poem in his daily prayers for its strength, mystery, and inspiration (translation by William Henthorne):

By Night

The light I saw when I awoke
Was from the torch that has no smoke;
The hill whose shade came through the wall
Has paid an unexpected call.
The music of the pine tree's wings
Comes from the harp that has no strings.
I see and hear the sight, the song;
Would I could pass its joy along!

Guided Imagery

As you observe your breath coming in, going out, notice how simple yet profound is the act of breathing. Notice the vessel of your body receiving the breath. Notice the space between exhalation and inhalation. Enter into that space. Enter and find yourself going on a journey—a journey to meet and visit with your mentor.

You find yourself in a place that feels comfortable and safe and vaguely familiar. You have visited here before, if only in your forgotten dreams or idle imaginings. Feel how genuine it is. Understand this is a place your mentor often visits.

Where are you? Inside or outside? Look around. What do you find? What time of day is it? What is the weather or ambience like? Are you in a home, a temple, a garden, a sacred space of wilderness?

Notice how safe you feel. Sense your anticipation. You are here to meet your mentor in his or her sanctuary. As your mentor approaches, notice how your energy shifts. Who comes? What is your mentor wearing, and what is the aura of energy like surrounding this being? You meet face to face. You can feel your energy auras touching. As your eyes meet, you feel your mentor's approval and acceptance. How does your mentor show caring and encouragement for who you are? You receive a special gift, a gift your mentor has been keeping safe just for you until the moment is right. Hold the gift, feel it. Of what is it made? Look at it carefully. Are there any symbols or words or glyphs on it?

Honor this special gift from your mentor. Deep inside of you, you feel this gift is right. You understand its implications. How do you express your gratitude? Listen and watch. How does your mentor respond?

And now it is time to return. Observe your breath as you prepare to go, holding and carrying your gift. Flow with your breath as it carries you back, back to the current time and place. Feel the surface beneath you. Feel the temperature and texture of the air. Hear the sounds around you. Notice the shift within you. Understand that you carry on the lineage of your mentor. Understand that your mentor is with you on your journey as teacher.

Journaling

Who is your mentor? Are you surprised? What special qualities does your mentor have that you also have? That you wish to cultivate? What is your gift? What do you wish to do to anchor this gift in everyday reality? How does this mentor help you become stronger yourself in your role of mentor/teacher/guide?

You as Inspired Teacher

Intention

In this journey you will find yourself as a teacher who draws from your inner source to inspire others to empower themselves through the maskmaking process.

Guided Imagery

You have just moved in Tiger's Breath Chi Kung. Now you sit or lie in relaxation. Feel your Microcosmic Orbit and chakras open and engaged. Feel the tingling of your inner awareness.

Breathe fully, deeply, easily. Feel your breath entering and gliding up the nasal passage. Feel the temperature of your breath as it climbs and changes. Feel how it changes as it enters into the portal of your third eye. How easily your breath passes through the lens of your third eye and into the center of your brain, then descends into the brainstem. As your breath descends, feel how it changes as it moves down into your throat and into your chest. Feel yourself descending, going deeper and deeper. You find yourself easily sinking into that spaciousness where there is no time, no distance.

You find yourself descending—into your heart, then down into the Tan Tien of your pelvis, where you find yourself centered and grounded, yet open and sensitive. You find your passion, passion that warms and invigorates you. You find your wisdom, wisdom that flows through your body as naturally as blood through your vessels, as naturally as Chi through your meridians.

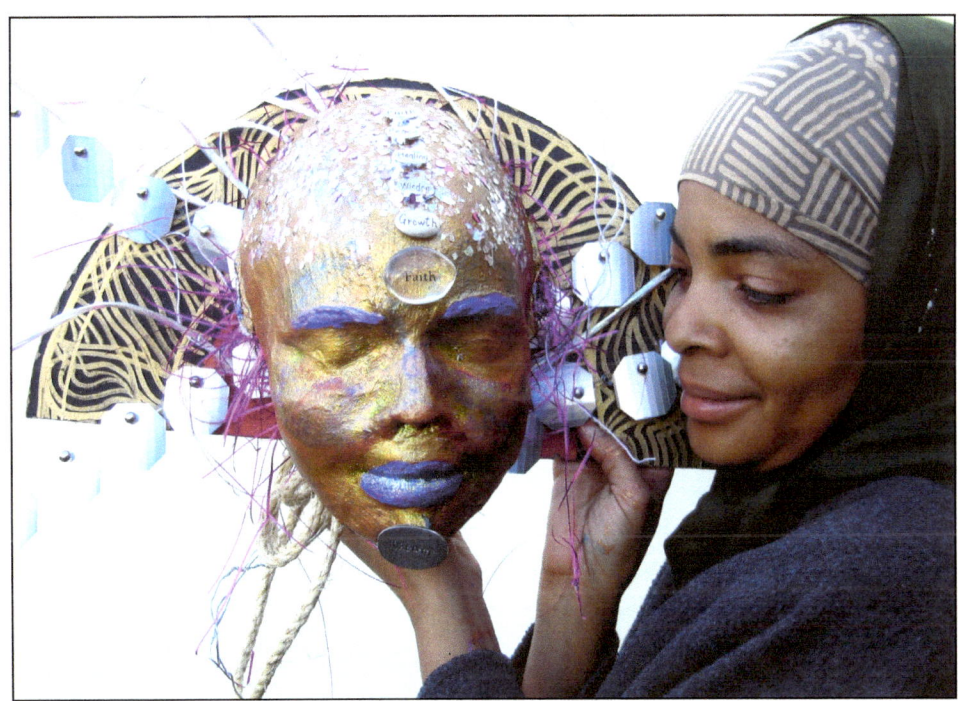

Aishah teaches art including maskmaking in a public school

You find yourself in a place of teaching, a sanctuary for learning. Are you inside or outside? What is the ambience of this place? Notice the presence and support of your mentor.

Listen to the sounds of your students. How many students are there? What is the age group?

Notice that some appear excited, some cautious, some happily interacting with others, some meditatively alone, but most appear open and ready to receive your gift of teaching.

Notice how you have set up this place of learning to fit your needs. Look at the art supplies, how well arranged they are. Your demonstration table is ready for you. Everything is arranged so that it feels like a vessel that holds and supports your creative maskmaking process.

The students quiet down as you approach your demonstration table. Notice the presence and support of your mentor. Feel your anticipation, the excitement of sharing your wisdom, of touching others in your own personal and caring way.

What is the message that you wish to share with them, from your heart, in your way, your style? How easily the teaching flows when you come from your heart! Feel the presence and reassurance of your mentor. Draw from within, from your center. Feel your passion, your ability to connect, to guide. In your unique way, draw from your own gifts and your own life experience. See yourself teaching, encouraging, inspiring. Look at the faces of your students as they receive, understand, and create in their own ways. See the light in their eyes as they surrender to the muse and empower themselves through creativity.

Then as you inhale, find yourself ascending from your Tan Tien up to the sanctum of your heart, up through your throat, and up into the spaciousness behind your third eye. In this space anything is possible. Let limitless possibility usher you back into the current time and place.

Journaling

What emotions come up in you as you find yourself preparing to teach and witnessing the range of students before you? What strengths and vulnerabilities are you aware of within you? How does the presence of your mentor support you?

Creating Sacred Space

There are two essential elements under your influence in creating sacred space.

One is the physical environment.

The other is you.

Physical Environment

Physical factors that influence the art setting include the following:

- Room size, layout, floors, and walls (for hanging the masks)

- Lighting, ambient noise, smell, temperature

- Seating and tables

- Accessible water, sinks, bathrooms

- Outdoor environment

It is wonderful if you have the perfect milieu for teaching. What is your dream space?

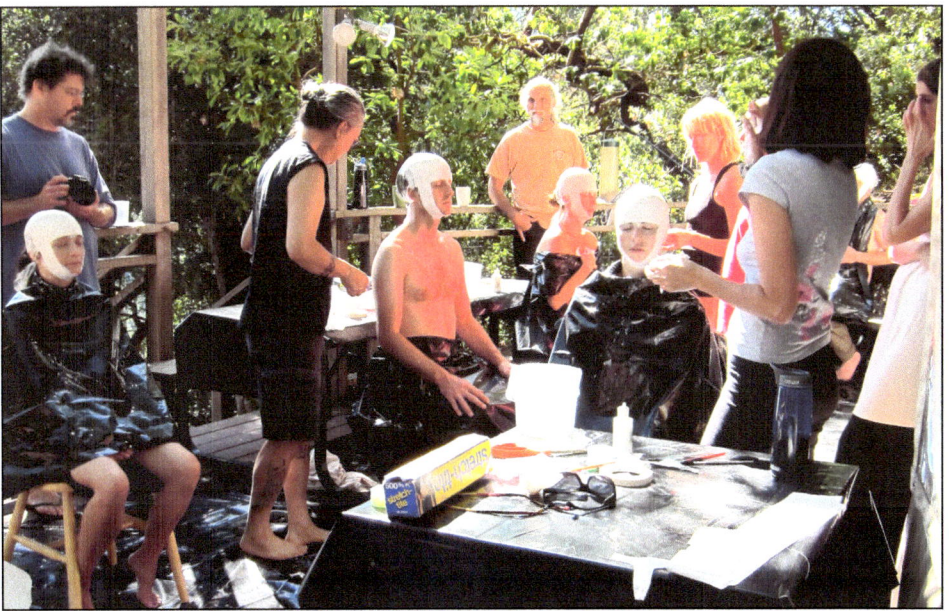

Faces of Your Soul at Luminous Body Integral School of Energy Medicine, Santa Cruz

Imagine

You are at the head of the room about to begin teaching. Students are gathered in a circle and sit ready and eager on meditation cushions. Tables and chairs wait in the background, ready to be arranged for maskmaking. The room is large and quiet with clear but gentle lighting adapted by rheostats. The hardwood floor is covered by a nice clean, comfortable carpet. At the end of the room is a large art sink with hot and cold running water. The walls are covered with freshly painted white art board ready to receive new art projects. Dark drapes wait to be pulled over large windows to provide darkness for a slide presentation or guided imagery journey. It is a warm day and the windows are open. There is a good possibility of making the mask molds in dappled sunlight on the deck outside. A gentle breeze carries in the fresh fertile aromas of the surrounding redwood forest. A Steller's jay chirps. Squirrels chatter. An occasional deer wanders by.

Reality

There is the ideal, and then there is reality and how you adjust to its quirks.

Although you will want to leave the room as you found it or better, spending some time adjusting it to your needs can make for a happier process. You can make the most of a small room by removing unnecessary furniture and wall decorations. You can darken a room with tarps over windows for slide presentation or guided imagery. You can invite students to bring their own pillows and blankets for comfort during guided imagery journeys. You can disguise ambient noise with gentle music (bring a digital music player or portable compact disc player and your favorite meditation and art-making music). You can create favorable aromas with incense (although be aware, some students may have sensitivities). You should cover floors, walls, and tables to protect them for art-making. You can bring an electric kettle to heat water if no hot water is available. If there is no water in the room, you can bring containers to haul it from the nearest source. You can bring portable fans if the room is too stuffy or heaters if it is too cold.

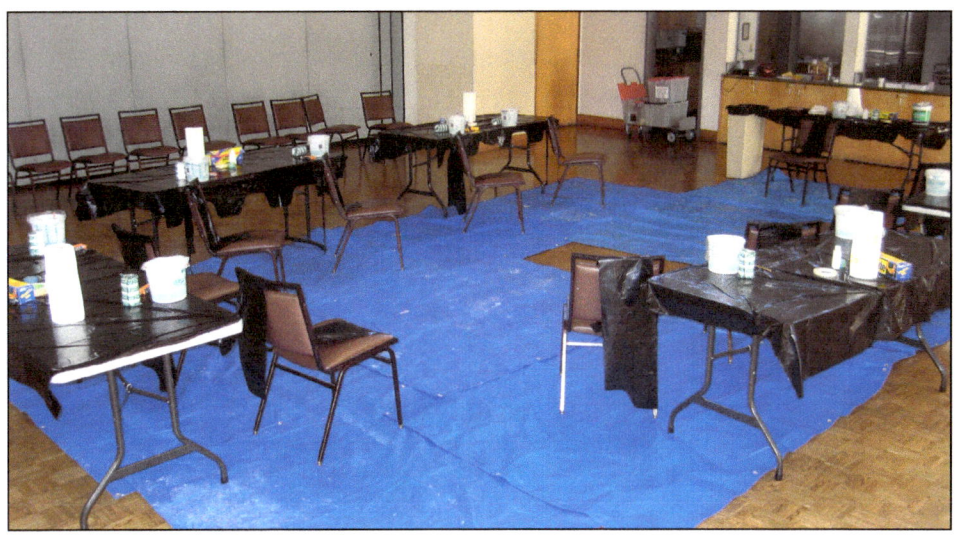

Setup for a class of 22 students

Remember: When you set up the room, there will be two demonstrations for two groups (Group A maskmakers and Group B maskgivers, then switch). For a class of sixteen students, you need to set up your demonstration table for one student plus partner (who can help with the demonstration) and seven places for the other seven pairs of students. The photo following is of a room set up for 22 students. Ten places are set up at tables in a horseshoe shape facing the demonstration table in front. There is plenty of space between tables. The floors are covered with tarp, the tables with plastic. Everything is ready for the students. Each chair (draped with a plastic bag to cover the maskgiver's clothes) is about two feet in front of the table with adequate space between each pair (usually we put two pairs at a six foot table). There are three large wastebaskets and easy access to bathrooms and sinks with hot and cold water. There are enough electrical outlets and extension cords so that students can have their own glue guns, plus enough tables and chairs for the painting and decorating process.

You

The other essential component to creating sacred space is your presence. This aspect is more elusive, and it is less about what you do than how you are. This is something for you to think about, to journal about, to envision.

Journaling

In your journal play with your responses to the following questions. What have you learned about yourself from previous experiences leading groups? What are your strengths as a group leader and teacher? What are your vulnerabilities? What do you love about teaching? What do you fear?

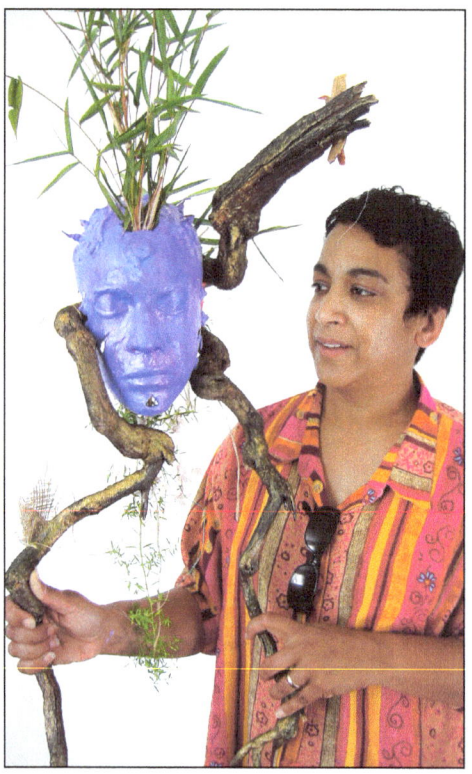

Yasmin: Ancestral Roots

Imagine yourself about ready to begin teaching your first maskmaking workshop. What qualities do you want to bring to the process? A calm, meditative, nurturing, yet strong and encouraging presence? Confidence combined with permissiveness, leadership combined with hospitality? Describe what happens as you lead the class. What are you like and how does the class respond? What challenges do you encounter and how do you handle them? What joys do you experience and how do you share them? What are the expressions on your students' faces at the end of the workshop?

Later on, after you have taught your first workshop, go back and read what you just wrote. See how it compares to what happened in reality. Look at the photos you have taken of the students and their masks. Are the images what you had imagined?

Complementary Written Materials

We recommend using, along with *Faces of Your Soul*, the following written materials: Flyer, Studio Considerations, Photo Permission/Mailing List, and Syllabus. The contents can be modified as needed.

Flyer

When you are ready to advertise your class, you will want a flyer announcing the class contents, date, time, location, and fee. You will want your flyer to be an invitation, readable and attractive, alluring and inspiring. Think about the types of participants you want to attract. What would entice them to look at the flyer, then to want to join the class? You may include an image of a mask or a person with her mask to arouse personal interest. You may use colored paper or ink to titillate one's muse. You may include a brief testimonial from a student as to the transformative value of the class. If the audience is unfamiliar with you, include a short biography of yourself. But remember to focus the information. A flyer that is too cluttered to read is like a room crammed with too much furniture. The mind does not even want to try to enter. Draw on your own personal creative, aesthetic, and communication skills to create a flyer that sings!

See "Sample Flyer: Your Warrior-Healer Mask" on page 72.

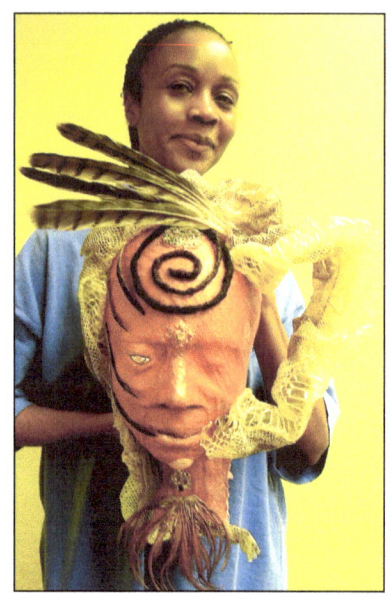

Annette: Snake's Wisdom

Studio Considerations

We also like to give students a set of guidelines for safe and considerate use of the art studio. In the thrill of creative discovery, it is easy for participants to get transported into a state of heightened enthusiasm. The guidelines remind them that they are sharing the room and process with others. When all is weighed, there is more expansion gained than freedom lost from sharing creative exploration and expression.

See "Sample Handout: Studio Considerations" on page 73.

Photo Permission/Mailing List

You will also want to have a Photo Permission/Mailing List for students to sign. This will provide you the means to keep in touch and send them photos of their masks and allow you to share your photos of their experience with others. Students are often greatly inspired by a slide presentation, whereby the images and stories of others' maskmaking experiences stimulate their own creativity. You can also use students' photos for promotion of your classes in advertising—on flyers, on your website, and on the internet.

See "Sample: Photo Permission/Mailing List" on page 75.

Syllabus

When designing a syllabus, we allow at very minimum six hours total for the maskmaking class (not including lunch and preparation time). This is a bare-bones class. An intimate group of five people might need a half hour for introductions, then two-and-a-half hours to make the mask molds. During lunch, light textures with spackling can be added, and the masks can be dried in a microwave oven. Then follow two-and-a-half hours of art demonstration and painting and decorating, then one-half hour of sharing. Realize that, the larger the class, the more time the process takes.

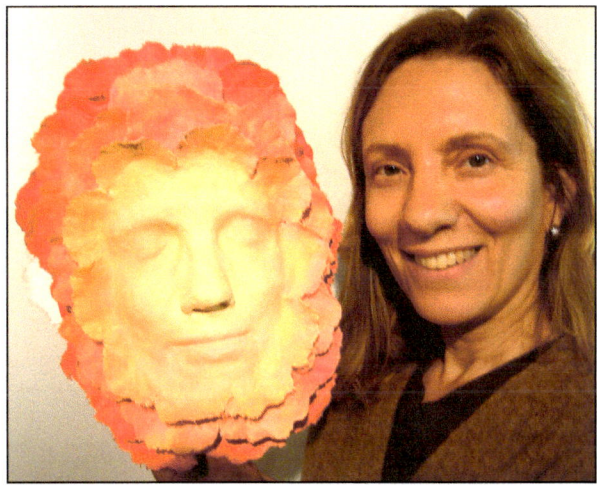

Kaaren: La Rose

In any class you must allow time after making the mask molds for drying them. This can be done during a long lunch break, if you have access to a conventional or microwave oven, or overnight.

If you have the luxury of more time, you can facilitate a fuller, richer, more rewarding experience. A workshop of two eight hour days works nicely for many groups. We also teach longer classes, in which we are able to offer more meditative movement, inner journey work, art-as-process, and discussion.

The following syllabi for one (minimum), two, and four day maskmaking workshops are samples for you to follow. The one day workshop is intense and focused, whereas the four day workshop is a depth experience, with more time for Chi Kung, guided imagery processes, a drawing/collage experience, and group sharing. Also included are suggestions for maskmaking in middle and high schools.

The theme you choose depends on your target group. With teens we have done work with Ancestors or on self-discovery. We have done Spirit Guide masks as an initiation to mark graduation from high school and entry into a new phase of life. With healing arts professionals, such as bodyworkers, energy healers, medical practitioners, counselors, social workers, and psychotherapists, we often evoke masks of the Inner Warrior-Healer. With groups on retreat in a wilderness setting, we may offer Totem Animal masks. With groups of participants whose focus is the spiritual search, we might summon masks of the Divine Within.

In workshops there are usually some people bored with their routines or dissatisfied with their jobs, who want to experience a sense of freedom, spontaneity, and joy. Some people feel divorced from their emotions and their bodies and want to reintegrate the mind with the body and the soul. Some are facing crucial decisions or turning points in their lives. Whatever the motivation, the "Faces of Your Soul" process is about supporting others in their journeys to discover their inner wisdom, their source, and their empowerment.

As you design your syllabus, consider the interests, needs, and life issues of the group. In your workshop you may invoke archetypes to support the life journeys of the group. You may lead a women-only group to discover "The Goddess Within." You may lead a men-only group to invoke the inner hero. You may want to lead a group of astrologists in making zodiac masks. You may design a workshop for corporate executives creating masks of leadership. You may create a Halloween/Day of the Dead workshop for children or adults that gives new and deeper meaning to the tradition of donning masks and costumes and inviting spooky presences and awareness beyond-the-grave. What kind of guided journeys would you create to bring the theme to life in the inner worlds of the participants? What unique art supplies might you include to inspire them?

See "One-day Syllabus: Your Mask of Ancestral Sources" on page 31, "Two-day Syllabus: Mask of Your Inner Warrior-Healer" on page 34, and "Four-day Syllabus: Your Totem Animal Mask" on page 36.

One-day Syllabus: Your Mask of Ancestral Sources

Title of Class

Instructor(s) and contact information (email, website, phone number). Name of educational institution, location, and units of credit, if applicable. Date and time of class.

Description

Discover your ancestral sources and create your own unique ancestor mask. Guided imagery and maskmaking are ancient, ubiquitous practices that evoke ancestral influences waiting to bring inspiration, connectedness, and depth to your creative explorations. Whether your ancestral sources are genetic, ethnic, spiritual, geographical, or cultural, guided imagery leads you into the realms of your psyche to connect with the ancestors and their lessons and wisdom. Then, through sculpting, painting, and embellishing a plaster gauze mold of your face, your Ancestor mask emerges. This experience is perfect for anyone interested in tapping the mysteries of the ancestors and creativity as a journey of self-discovery. No art experience needed.

Registration

Fee: $____—includes a feast of art supplies (25 colors of acrylic paint, tools, beads, furs, feathers, fabric, natural materials, herbs, etc.). Please collect and bring personal items for your mask (e.g., locks of hair, special mementos, photos, jewelry, etc.). One student incorporated his newborn's umbilical cord on his mask; another, her grown children's baby teeth. One woman turned her mask into an altar and planted ashes of her beloved dog inside.

Space is limited. Email or call ASAP (phone number, email address). To reserve your space, a $____ nonrefundable deposit is required.

View students and their masks: www.flickr.com/photos/kaleoching.

View *Tao of Creativity* maskmaking video: www.kaleoching.com

Recommended Reading: *Faces of Your Soul: Rituals in Art, Maskmaking, and Guided Imagery with Ancestors, Spirit Guides, and Totem Animals* by Elise and Kaleo Ching (North Atlantic Books, 2006). In bookstores or Amazon.com. Before class, please read Spirit Guides (pp. 9-49), Ancestors (79-113), and photos/instructions on making mask molds (115-140). The reading enhances your understanding and trust so you can experience more freedom and depth in your technical and creative processes.

Date (9:30 am–6:00 pm)

Please be prompt. Please bring bag lunch. Wear grubby clothes. Remove contact lenses for maskmaking. If you have a journal/sketch book, please bring it.

9:30 am	Opening circle and guided imagery (Meeting Your Ancestral Guide)
10:15	Maskmaking demonstration [by teacher] while group A makes masks of partners in group B, then break
11:30	Maskmaking demonstration [by teacher] while group B makes masks of partners in group A
12:30 pm	Filling the nostrils, clean-up
1:00	Lunch (drying masks)
1:45	Art demonstration; painting and decorating your Ancestor mask
5:00	Clean-up, sharing circle, documenting with photos

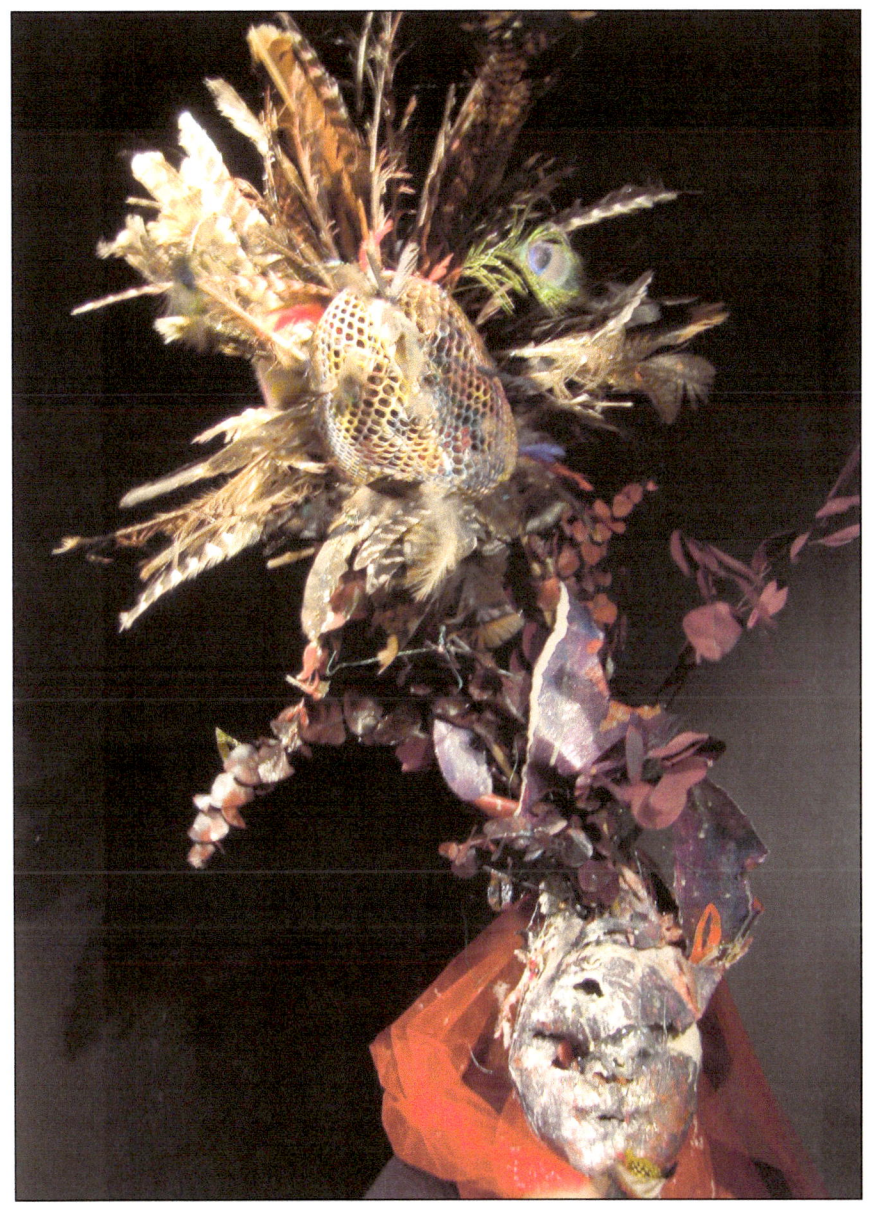

Elizabeth's ancestral mask ritual at JFK University

Two-day Syllabus: Mask of Your Inner Warrior-Healer

Title of Class

Instructor(s) and contact information (email, website, phone number). Name of educational institution, location, and units of credit, if applicable. Dates and times of class.

Description

Discover your Inner Warrior-Healer and create your own unique totem mask. Chi Kung, guided imagery, and maskmaking are ancient and ubiquitous practices that summon archetypes, latent or raw, within the psyche, to emerge as creative expressions of personal as well as universal themes and meanings. In this exciting workshop you will experience an initiation of manifesting and empowering your relationship with your inner Warrior-Healer. The journey begins with Chi Kung to open your body and its energy vortices and to encourage creativity and self-expression. Guided imagery leads you deeper into the realms of your psyche to connect with your inner wisdom. Then, through sculpting, painting, and embellishing a plaster gauze mold of your face, your Warrior-Healer mask of personal transformation emerges. This experience is perfect for artists, therapists, healers, and anyone interested in the mysteries of energy flows, archetypal influences, and creativity as a journey of self-discovery and healing. No art or Chi Kung experience needed.

Registration

Fee: $_____—includes a feast of art supplies (25 colors of acrylic paint, tools, beads, furs, feathers, fabric, natural materials, herbs, etc.). Please collect and bring personal items for your mask (e.g., locks of hair, special mementos, photos, jewelry, etc.). One student incorporated his newborn's umbilical cord on his mask; another, her grown children's baby teeth. One woman turned her mask into an altar and planted ashes of her beloved dog inside.

Space is limited. Email or call ASAP (phone number, email address). To reserve your space, a $_____ nonrefundable deposit is required.

View students and their masks: www.flickr.com/photos/kaleoching.

View *Tao of Creativity* maskmaking video: www.kaleoching.com.

Recommended Reading: *Faces of Your Soul: Rituals in Art, Maskmaking, and Guided Imagery with Ancestors, Spirit Guides, and Totem Animals* by Elise and Kaleo Ching (North Atlantic Books, 2006). In bookstores or Amazon.com. Before class, please read Spirit Guides (pp. 9-49), Mask of Your Warrior-Healer (151-154), and photos/instructions on making mask molds (115-140). The reading enhances your understanding and trust so you can experience more freedom and depth in your technical and creative processes.

Day One (10 am–6 pm)

Please be prompt. Please bring bag lunch. Wear grubby clothes. Remove contact lenses for maskmaking. If you have a journal/sketch book, please bring it.

10 am	Opening circle—introductions, slide presentation
11:00	Tiger's Breath Chi Kung
Noon	Guided imagery (Meeting Your Inner Warrior-Healer) and journaling
1:00	Lunch
2:00	Making your mask mold. Please be prompt! Maskmaking demonstration [by teacher] while group A makes masks of partners in group B, then break
3:30	Maskmaking demonstration [by teacher] while group B makes masks of partners in group A
4:30	Filling the nostrils, using media for creating texture or smoothness, clean-up
5:30	Sharing, guidelines for explorations with your Warrior-Healer, dream awareness

Day Two (10 am–6 pm)

Please bring bag lunch. Please be prompt.

10 am	Chi Kung: Tiger's breath
10:30	Guided imagery (Ritual with Your Warrior-Healer)
11:00	Art demo: painting & decorating
11:30	Painting and decorating your Warrior-Healer mask (eat bag lunch as desired)
5 pm	Clean-up, sharing circle, documenting with photos

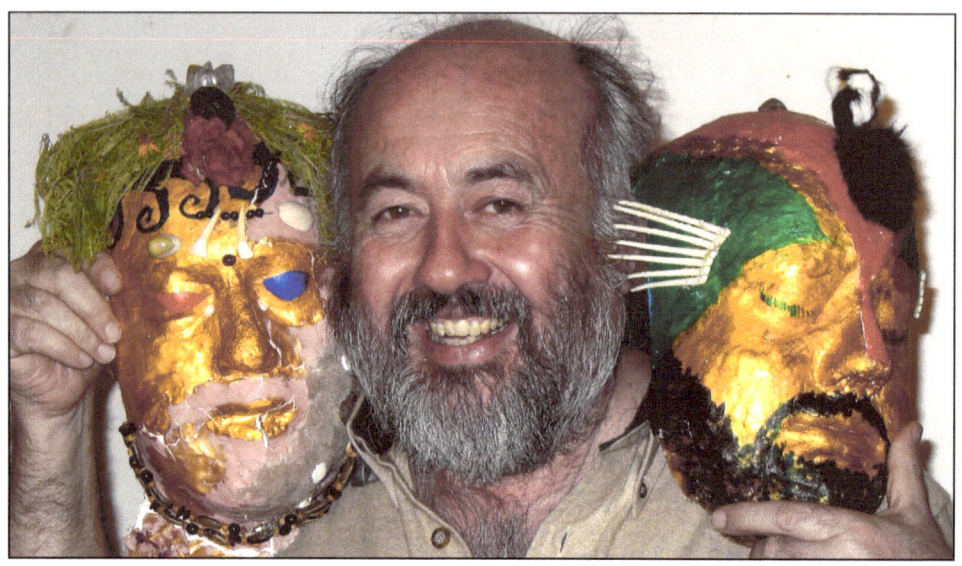

Gilles, Warrior-Healer: From Two Workshops Integrating Chi Nei Tsang and Maskmaking
(with Gilles Marin, Kaleo, and Elise)

Four-day Syllabus: Your Totem Animal Mask

Title of Class

Instructor(s) and contact information (email, website, phone number). Name of educational institution, location, and units of credit, if applicable. Dates and times of class.

Description

Meet your personal totem animal (power animal), who is waiting to connect with you and accompany you on your creative life's journey. Your totem animal shares the wisdom and ways of its species and brings you a unique understanding of your place in the world of nature and of interrelatedness with others. It can help motivate and inspire you, enhance your intuition and sensitivity to your surroundings, and share its own life's lessons. The journey begins with Eight Animal Chi Kung to open your body and its energy vortices and to encourage creativity and self-expression. Guided imagery leads you deeper into the landscape of your psyche to connect with your personal totem animal. Then, through sculpting, painting, and embellishing a plaster gauze mold of your face, your totem animal mask emerges. This experience is perfect for artists, therapists, healers, spiritual seekers, and anyone interested in the mysteries of totem animals, energy flows, and creativity as a journey of self-discovery and healing. No art or Chi Kung experience needed.

Registration

Fee: $____—includes a feast of art supplies (25 colors of acrylic paint, tools, beads, furs, feathers, fabric, natural materials, herbs, etc.). Please collect and bring personal items for your mask (e.g., locks of hair, special mementos, photos, jewelry, etc.). One student incorporated his newborn's umbilical cord on his mask; another, her grown children's baby teeth. One woman turned her mask into an altar and planted ashes of her beloved dog inside.

Space is limited. Email or call ASAP (phone number, email address). To reserve your space, a $____ nonrefundable deposit is required.

View students and their masks: www.flickr.com/photos/kaleoching.

View *Tao of Creativity* maskmaking video: www.kaleoching.com.

Recommended reading: *Faces of Your Soul: Rituals in Art, Maskmaking, and Guided Imagery with Ancestors, Spirit Guides, and Totem Animals* by Elise and Kaleo Ching (North Atlantic Books, 2006). In bookstores or www.Amazon.com. Before class, please read Spirit Guides (pp. 9-49), Totem Animal (51-78), and photos/instructions on making mask molds (115-140). The reading enhances your understanding and trust so you can experience more freedom and depth in your technical and creative processes.

Day One (10 am–6 pm)

Please be prompt. Bring bag lunch. Bring journal/sketch book.

10 am	Opening circle—introductions, slide presentation
11:00	Chi Kung: Chi ball; body, mind, spirit Tan Tiens; transmit/absorb Chi; scan hair, face, skin; Eight Animal Chi Kung
Noon	Lunch
1:30	Guided imagery (Journey to the Lower World), journaling

2:00	Collage/drawing art demonstration
2:30	Collage/drawing (Journey to the Lower World)
3:30	Guided imagery (Meeting Your Totem Animal), journaling
4:00	Collage/drawing (Totem Animal)
5:00	Clean up, sharing, guidelines for mask mold sculpting on day two, review Chi Kung

Day Two (10 am–6 pm)

Please be prompt. Please bring bag lunch. Wear grubby clothes. Remove contact lenses for maskmaking. Bring journal/sketch book.

10 am	Chi Kung: review, moving as your Totem Animal
11:00	Guided imagery (Merging with Your Totem Animal), journaling
11:30	Collage/drawing (You and Totem Animal as One), clean up
1 pm	Lunch
2:00	Making your mask mold. Please be prompt! Maskmaking demonstration [by teacher] while group A makes masks of partners in group B, then break
3:30	Maskmaking demonstration [by teacher] while group B makes masks of partners in group A
4:30:	Filling the nostrils, using media for creating texture or smoothness, clean-up
5:30	Sharing, guidelines for explorations with your Totem Animal, dream awareness

Day Three (10 am–6 pm)

Please be prompt. Please bring bag lunch. Bring journal/sketch book.

10 am	Chi Kung
11:00	Guided imagery (Nest/Den of Your Totem Animal), journaling
11:30	Art demo: painting and decorating your Totem Animal mask, sculpting nest/den
12 pm	Painting and decorating your Totem Animal mask (eat bag lunch as desired)
5:30	Clean up

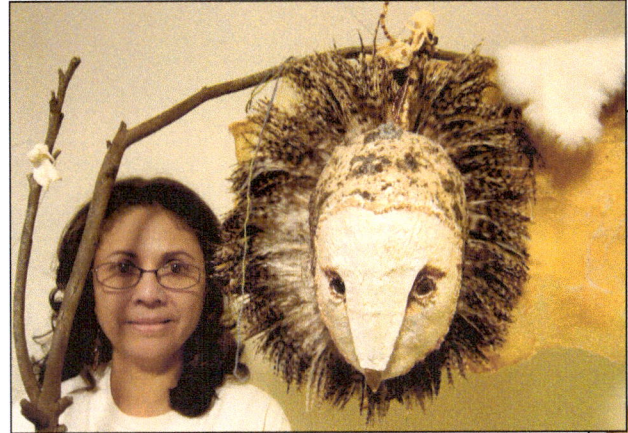

Michelle: Barn Owl

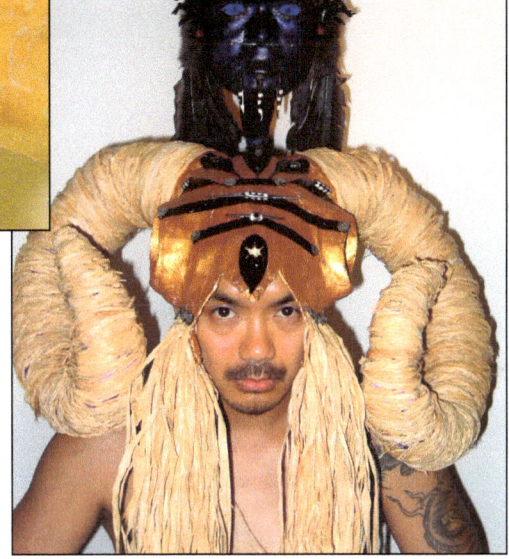

Raven: Ram

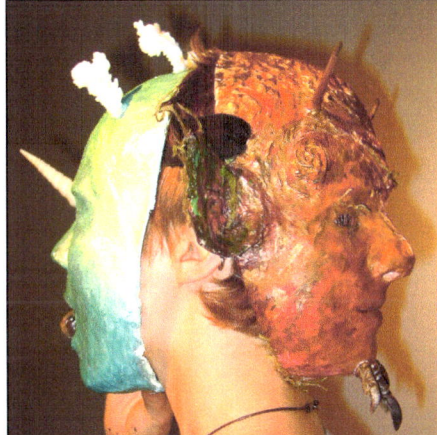

Sonja: Creatures of Forest and Sea

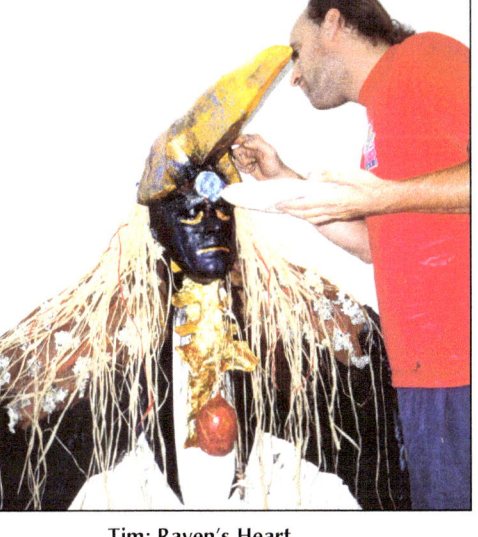

Tim: Raven's Heart

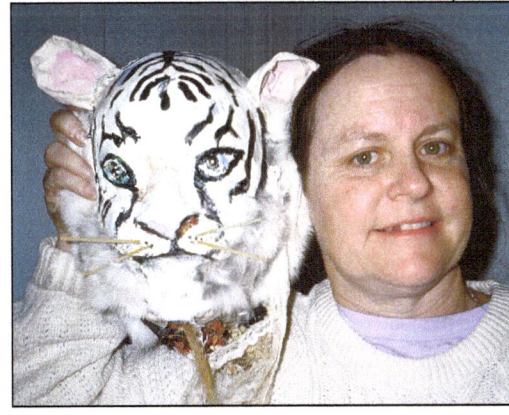

Shirley: White Tiger

Day Four (10 am–6 pm)

Please be prompt. Please bring bag lunch. Bring journal/sketch book.

10 am	Chi Kung
11:00	Guided imagery (Totem Animal and You Confront an Adversary), journaling
Noon	Finish painting and decorating your Totem Animal mask, sculpting adversary, nest/den, power objects, medicine pouch, shield (eat bag lunch as desired)
5 pm	Clean-up, sharing circle, documenting with photos

Maskmaking in the Schools: Considerations and Syllabus

Considerations

Our Chi Kung, guided imagery, and maskmaking process can be a powerful addition to secondary school curricula. It is vehicle for creative learning through the mind, the heart, and the body. It shows students a way of learning through integration of the mental, emotional, and physical intelligences.

In many urban schools you will be teaching a diverse group of individuals with cultural, gender, religious, and language differences. In Oakland High, one teacher revealed there were 57 languages and dialects spoken. In any class there may be students dealing with serious life issues or special challenges. The maskmaking process can be a way for the students to find out more about who they are, where they feel they belong in our society, who their ancestors and parents are, and what their innermost wisdom is teaching them. It can encourage them to discover and connect with guides and helpers in life. Students may connect with their grandparents or distant ancestors, the Virgin of Guadalupe, Spiderman, Bella Swan, or Barack Obama. Homework can be part of this process. They can do research, interview someone, do a collage, collect meaningful embellishments for their masks, and do journaling.

In public schools or after-school programs, often time is limited. You may have two hours for each class. Sometimes the teacher can combine an English or History and an Art class or work it out so that you will have more time. Ask the teacher what he/she would like to see happen with this group of students and what is realistic in terms of what you can offer.

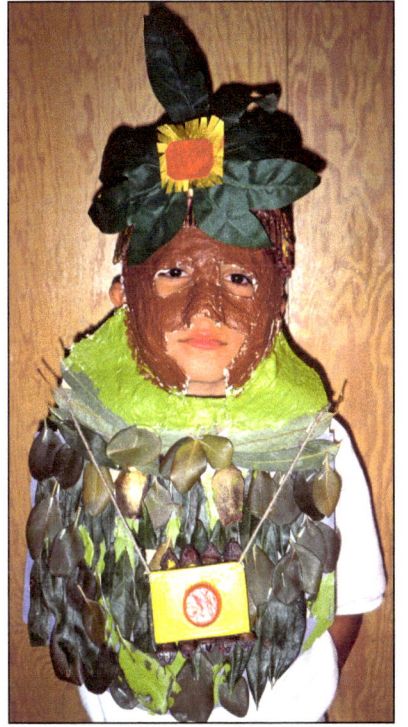

Miguel: 4th Grade

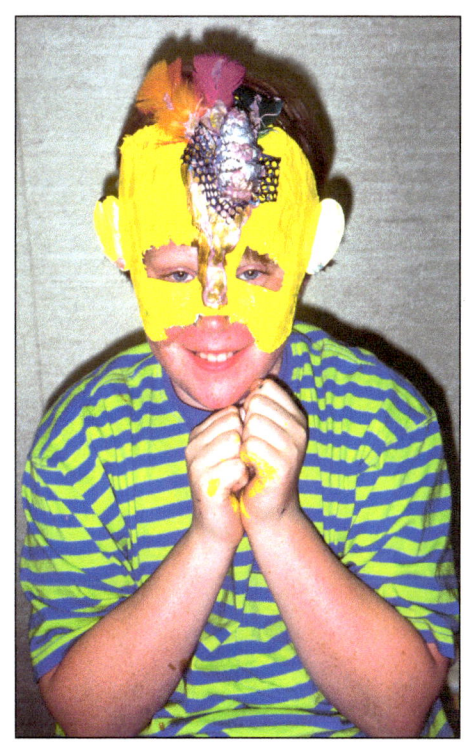

Daisy: 5th Grade

These classes work well if you have flexibility and collaborate with the teacher. The teacher can prepare students with a slide presentation of world cultural masks or by leading them in journal writing a day or two before you teach. Sometimes the teacher combines an English creative writing lesson or a mask-related lesson from Social Studies, History, or Art a few days before you come in to teach.

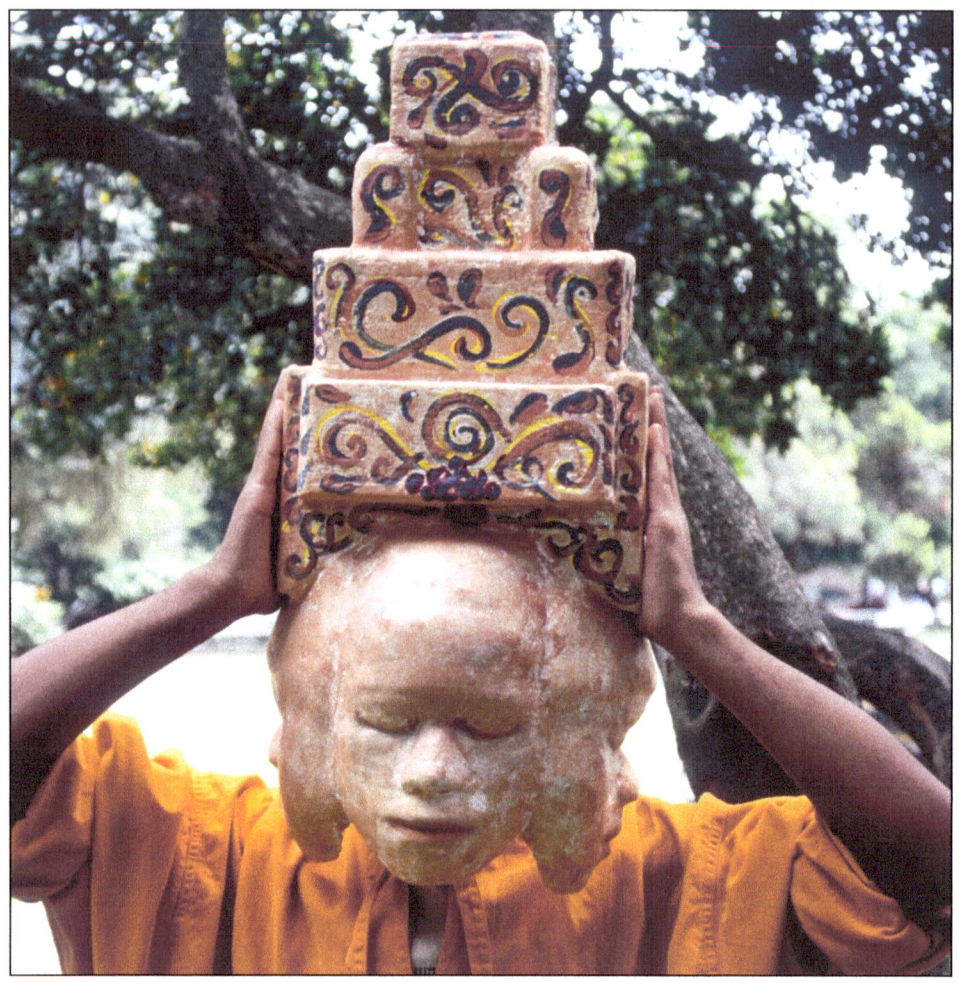

Tanawat: 11th Grade

It is very important that you are well prepared. What is your intention for the class? Remember this process is all about the students empowering themselves. Make sure you are confident and know your techniques well. You may have 30 students in class and only two hours to make mask molds. You need to have enough gauze (plan to bring extra rolls just in case) and all the right supplies. If you are working with grade school students, adjust and simplify the maskmakeing techniques by pre-cutting the gauze into one inch by three inch strips. Make it clear to the teacher and your assistants what you expect of them and how they can best help. Set up the room so that it is a vessel conducive for focus and creativity. Arrange the desks so students can see your demonstration clearly and you have a psychological vantage point for observing them.

Sample syllabus

1st Monday (2 hours)

Slide show, guided imagery, journal writing: Students can be assigned to journal during the week and to gather supplies to decorate their masks.

2nd Monday (2 hours)

Making the mask mold: Make sure you have assistants to help you set up and clean up. Everything must be set up and prepared for the students. Emphasize how important it is for them to focus and not be distracted. Start with group A, then do group B. They are to follow your instructions step by step. Once you start making the mask mold, they usually get very involved and fascinated. During the week the teacher can do guided imagery and other activities related to the process and encourage students to collect and bring personal things for decorating their masks.

3rd Monday (2 hours)

Painting and decorating the masks: Bring paints and necessary supplies, with an emphasis on interesting but low-cost materials.

Art Studio

Remember to bring the following additional aids to your class:

- Slides/projector or computer for an inspirational slide presentation
- Camera for documenting
- Cart to haul bins of supplies
- Digital audio player or portable compact disc player and music
- Bell to ring to break up noise and summon attention.

Sculpting the Mask Mold

The following guidelines refer to the *Faces of Your Soul* section, Practice: Sculpting the Mask, pp. 128-139.

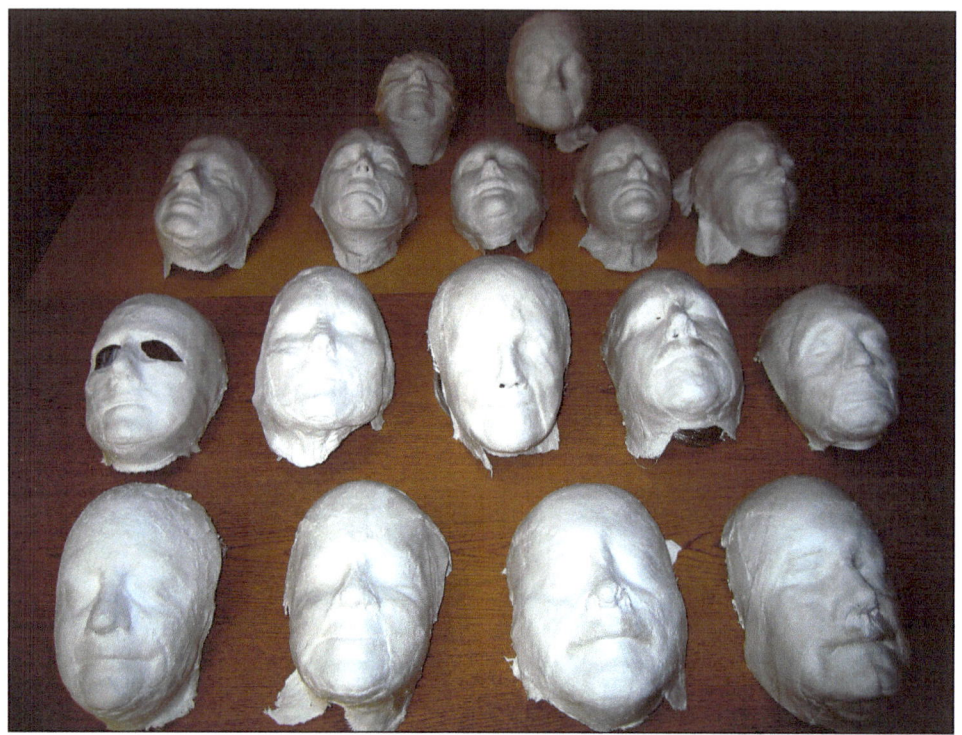

Mask molds drying

Mask Mold Sculpting Supplies

These are listed on p. 129 in *Faces of Your Soul,* but we will elaborate on them here.

- *Oil-based lotion to protect the maskgiver's face, under the chin* (or whatever surfaces the gauze will cover): Some students with allergies can bring their own lotion. Slather maskgivers copiously. The first layer usually absorbs, so encourage them to keep applying until a white layer is visible.

- *Petroleum jelly to apply to the eyelashes, any facial or stray scalp hairs:* Petroleum jelly should also go in copious amounts over the oil based lotion on beards and mustaches. Maskgivers should have taken out their contact lenses. If not, or if the maskgiver has an eye problem or sensitivity, an oval piece of plastic wrap needs to be cut to cover each eye. Otherwise, petroleum jelly should seal the eyelashes closed so that no plaster gets in the eyes. Once petroleum jelly is on, the maskgivers need to keep their eyes closed.

- *Clear plastic wrap to cover the ears and all scalp hair:* Cover like a shower cap. Tie or tape in place.

- *Plastic garbage bag to wear to protect the maskgiver's clothes:* This can be taped like a hair salon apron around the neck with a paper towel bib to catch trickling gauzy water. Recycle the bag for use on the second maskgiver. The maskmaker may also use a garbage bag as an apron if desired.

- *Plaster of Paris gauze roll (four inches wide by five yards long):* This is the same stuff used to cast broken limbs. Get the fast-acting kind. Usually one roll per participant is adequate.

- *Warm water, about dishwater temperature, in a bowl:* Bowls for warm gauze-dipping water. The water should not scald but needs to be plenty warm, as it cools down quickly.

- *Scissors:* Large sharp shears.

- *Masking tape:* To tape plastic wrap around head and garbage bag apron around neck.

- *Brushes (a small one and a medium size one):* These should be separate from the ones used for painting, be kept in water when not in use, and be washed thoroughly when no longer needed.

Also include the following:

- Tarps or coverings to protect tables and floor

- Paper towels or facial tissue

- Electric urn or kettle to heat water

- Trash cans lined with garbage bags (for disposal of plaster wiped from bowls and scissors and dirty plaster water; make sure absolutely no plaster goes into the sinks and plumbing)

- Spackling paste (interior/exterior) for textures on the masks

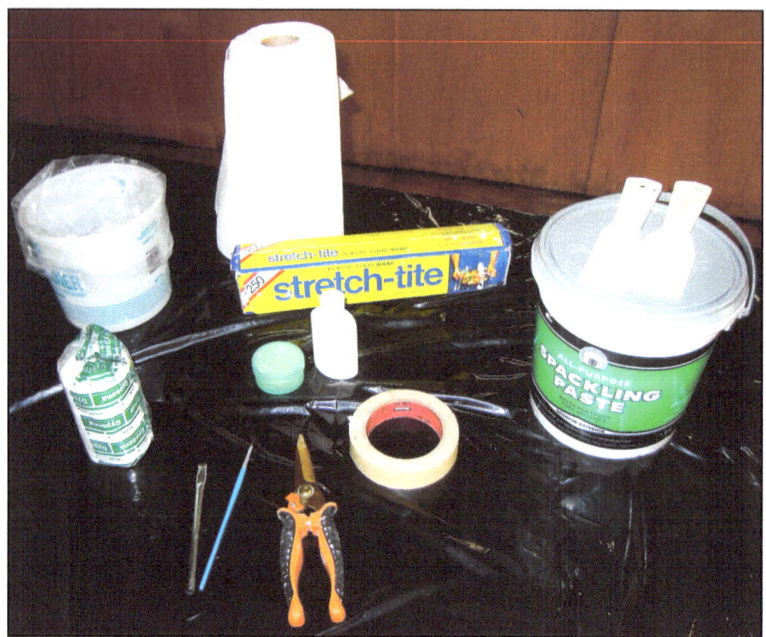

Supplies for making the mask mold

Reminders

The reminders for the maskmaking process are listed on p. 130 of *Faces of Your Soul*, but we will elaborate on them here.

- Maskgivers should remove any earrings, necklaces, and contact lenses. If contact lenses cannot be removed, do not cover eyelashes with petroleum jelly, but use an oval piece of plastic wrap to cover each eye. Make sure the entire eyelid line is covered so that no gauze gets in the eye. If piercing jewelry cannot come off, cover it with plenty of petroleum jelly.

- *Alway measure the gauze strips.* This means measure them in relation to the maskgiver's face. Allow a little extra for overlap.

- *Always double the gauze strip unless otherwise noted.* Double the head wrap lengthwise instead of widthwise (see steps 4, 5, and 6, *Faces of Your Soul* pp. 131-132). Do not double the 1/4 inch nose strip (see step 9, p. 133). After the mask is removed from the maskgiver's face, the cone-shaped pieces that insert in the nostril holes are also single layers (see step 21, p. 137). All other pieces are doubled widthwise.

- *Fold the gauze first; then, immerse in warm water.* This makes the gauze easier to handle. Once dipped in water, the gauze wrinkles easily. Additionally, always keep the cut gauze pieces away from the water, as accidental water drips or splashes can ruin the gauze for use.

- *Activate the plaster gauze by stroking it between your fingers.* You want the gauze to be moist, so do not stroke it too much, just enough so that it is dripping but not gushing water.

- *When applying the gauze strips, overlap them on the face. Then, smooth and massage the gauze gently with your fingers and palms or a brush.* You want to see the pores in the gauze fill and become white with plaster. Make sure to massage the junctures between gauze pieces thoroughly so that the mask will dry connected and strong.

- *All instructions refer to a four inch wide fold of gauze unless otherwise noted.* See above for exceptions.

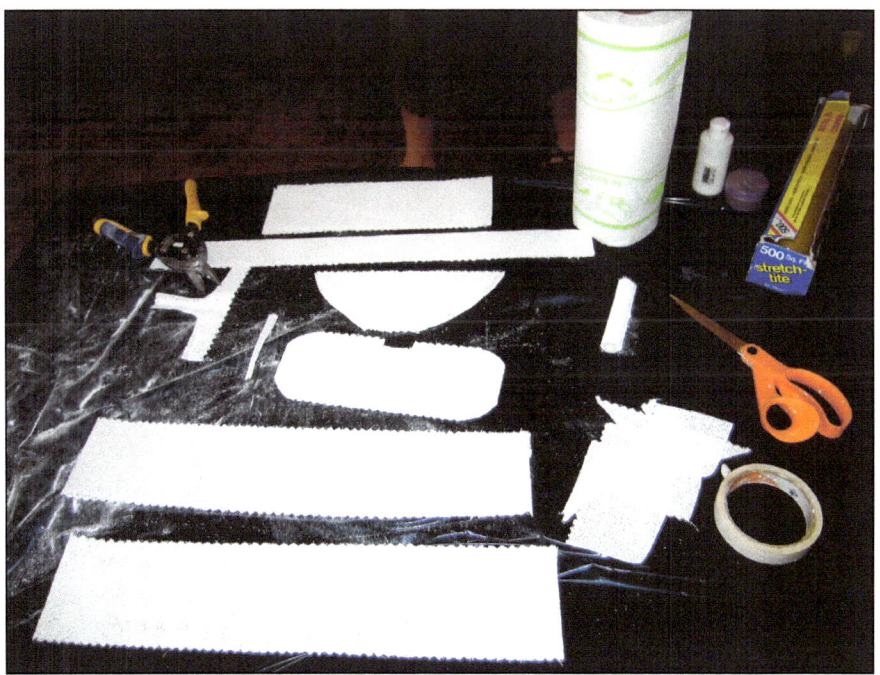

Gauze strips laid out and kept away from splashing water

Getting Ready for Sculpting the Mask Mold

When guiding others in sculpting the mask mold, we have found it works best to do two demonstrations, one for each group. You may choose to demonstrate on someone who has special needs or concerns. If there are an odd number of participants, you can demonstrate on the extra person during the first round. Then during the second round you can either make another mask of that person's face, or the maskgiver of another pair can assist you making the mask of his or her partner, while the extra person assists another maskmaking pair.

The beginning of the chapter, Sculpting the Mask, pp. 115-127, gives our guidelines for getting students physically and psychologically ready for the mask mold sculpting process.

You may have your own techniques you want to use. It is important for participants to feel connected with each other and safe and comfortable. You can facilitate this by making the environment as pleasing as possible. The lighting should be not too harsh, yet adequate for the maskmaker to see. The room temperature should be comfortably warm. The cooling gauze takes warmth away from the maskgiver, but the plastic garbage bag apron is warming. Maskgivers should be comfortable in their chairs so that they can sit still for 45 minutes. Space is important. For some people it is uncomfortable to be sitting with their eyes closed in a group of people and to be touched on their faces.

Maskmaking is a form of massage that affects the energetic, physical, emotional, mental, and spiritual bodies. The maskgivers should feel that they have room to breathe comfortably. There should be enough space around the chairs for the maskmakers to move around. You can play soothing music, like environmental sounds, meditation music, or melodious instrumentals.

Partners can get connected to each other through good communication. The maskgiver should let the maskmaker know of any concerns, physically or emotionally. The maskmaker can begin to introduce the maskgiver to receiving touch by helping apply the lotion and petroleum jelly to the maskgiver's face and, when they are both ready and waiting for the group to start, by offering a gentle shoulder and neck massage.

The maskgiver's job is to be still and receive. Many people find this a refreshing and liberating experience. How many times does one get to be safely quiet and receptive among a group of people? We have actually experienced maskgivers getting so relaxed from the facial massage that they fall asleep under the mask mold. The maskmaker's job is to follow carefully step by step your detailed guidance in maskmaking, keep pace with your lead, and at the same time remain sensitive to the maskgiver's responses and any signals of discomfort or distress.

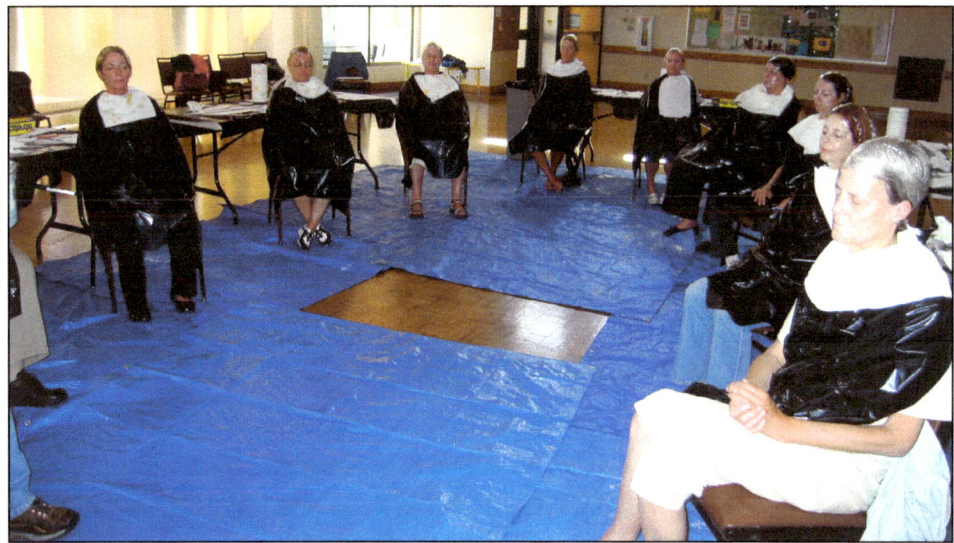

Wisdom University students ready to have their mask molds made

Kaleo's Journal

My experience with Rachel reminded me how important it is to be sensitive when you touch someone's lips or eyes. Rachel's breath quickened as her husband, John, smoothed the gauze strips over her eyes. Her nervous body was experiencing fright, and her breathing became rapid and shallow. John called me over to help. I immediately pressed my hands against acupressure points on the toes and balls of her feet. The energy sank into the earth, and her breathing calmed. I reassured her, "Rachel, if you want, I can remove the mask from your face in a second. However, please consider that it may be beneficial for you personally to keep moving into the process. I'll inform you exactly what each next step will be. Would you like me to continue?" Rachel nodded her head. As I continued making the mask, I talked to her, defining each step. She communicated to me that it was okay through the calming of her breath and the relaxation of her body. After the experience Rachel looked triumphant and shared with John and me that her fear was about her childhood sexual and psychological abuse from her father. She said staying with and through her anxiety to the calmness at the other side, with the safety and support of the presence of two men whose touch she could trust, helped her to reach a new level of healing and integration.

Dealing with a Maskgiver's Anxiety, Fears, or Concerns

Usually people find the experience of being the maskgiver to be interesting, sometimes pleasant, often meditative. But sometimes fears come up. These can be related to previous experiences of physical or emotional trauma, health issues such as difficulty breathing from asthma or eye, skin, or respiratory allergies, or more generalized insecurity or anxiety.

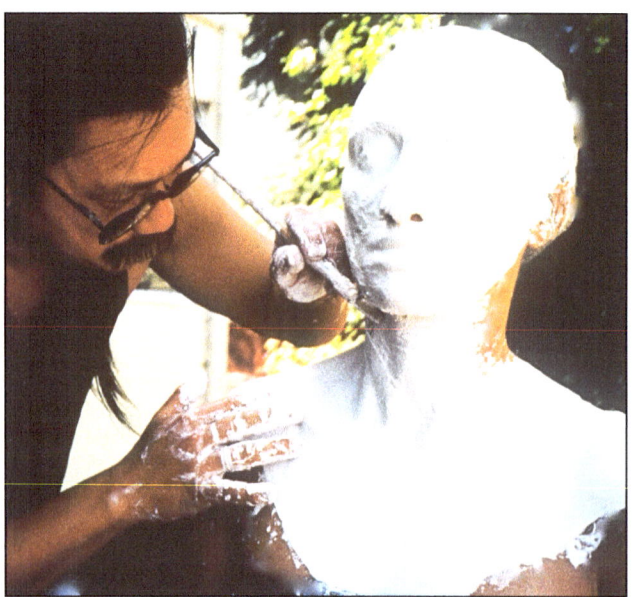

Reassuring the maskgiver with voice and touch

Whatever the source, *it is important to reassure maskgivers before the process begins that the process is safe and that the mask mold can be removed in seconds if need be.* Rarely have we found, in the thousands of masks we have guided people in making, that this is necessary. But it is important for maskgivers to know they are free to end the process at any time just by signaling the partner to remove the mold. Then if maskgivers have any special concerns, they should share these with their partners and the teacher. If the eyes are an issue, the gauze can be tailor-cut to encircle the eyes rather than covering them so that the maskgiver's eyes can remain open. If the maskgiver is a mouth-breather, the gauze can be cut so that there is an opening between the lips. If general anxiety is an issue, the maskmaker can employ a calm but confident approach and help the maskgiver to relax with a neck and shoulder massage engaging acupressure points (pp. 120-127) prior to beginning the process and by using a soothing tone of voice.

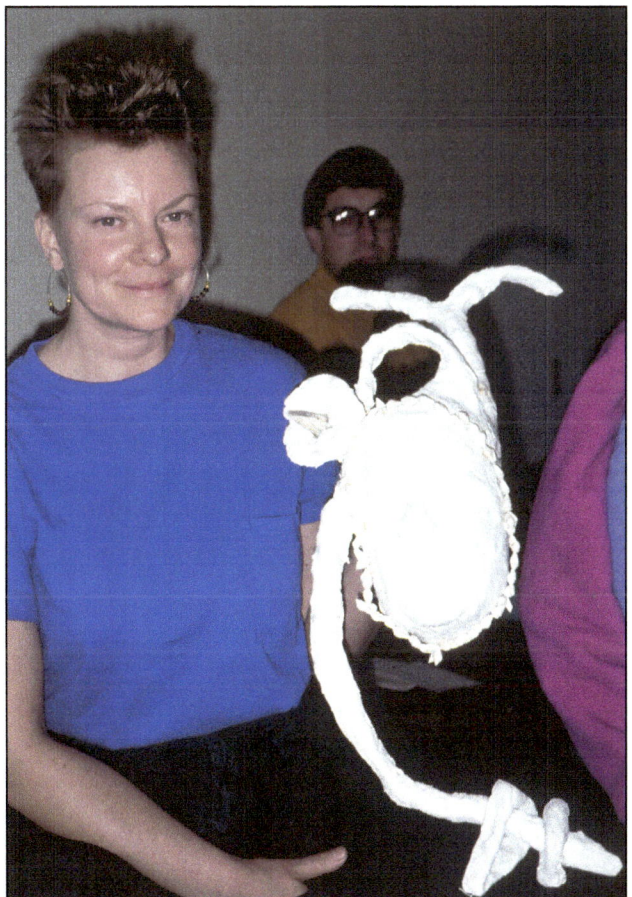

Carolyn: Mask-sculpture

When the masks are peeled off, some maskgivers feel like an eggshell has opened and a new birth has occurred. Some feel like a burden has been lifted and new freedom awaits. It is interesting to watch them as they hold their masks. Over the years we have witnessed a few people crush their masks in a violent surge of emotion. Later, they worked with the crushed gauze, cutting or molding it into meaningful sculptures. Many look at their masks with excitement and embrace their masks in respect and awe. As they look at their masks, they recognize parents, grandparents, or distant ancestors. Stages of life—childhood, adolescence, young adulthood, parenthood, grandparenthood—may appear. Dreams take shape. Archetypes emerge. The masks are like fresh soil waiting to nourish new life.

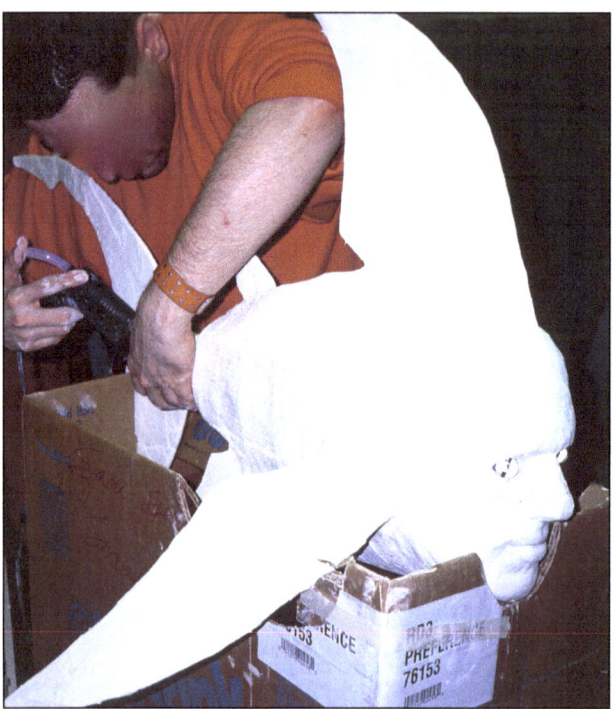

County Jail Inmate

Once the masks are dry, it is the time for the maskgivers to create forms if desired. You as teacher may prompt them with encouraging questions:

What did you see in the guided imagery? Was it the sun? An old oak tree? A geometric shape? A horned mythological creature? Does it ask for more sculpting? What might you use—cardboard, more plaster gauze, foam core, plastic, wood, wire, newspaper? And how do you wish to sculpt? Listen to your soul. It may inspire you to cut precisely with metal shears or blades and construct a form or to rip, tear, and peel with your hands to destroy then reconstruct.

It may call you to add plaster gauze or lather spackling or modeling paste to shape eyebrows, ears, or beards, to create a surface in which to inscribe words or symbols, or to smooth over the surface of the mask mold. Or you may be urged to puncture with the awl, sew with sinew, or velcro shapes together. You may be called to hammer in nails, cut openings for eyes or antlers, or open and part the lips. As you feel the fertile contours of the landscape of your mask mold, dialogue with the images that appear.

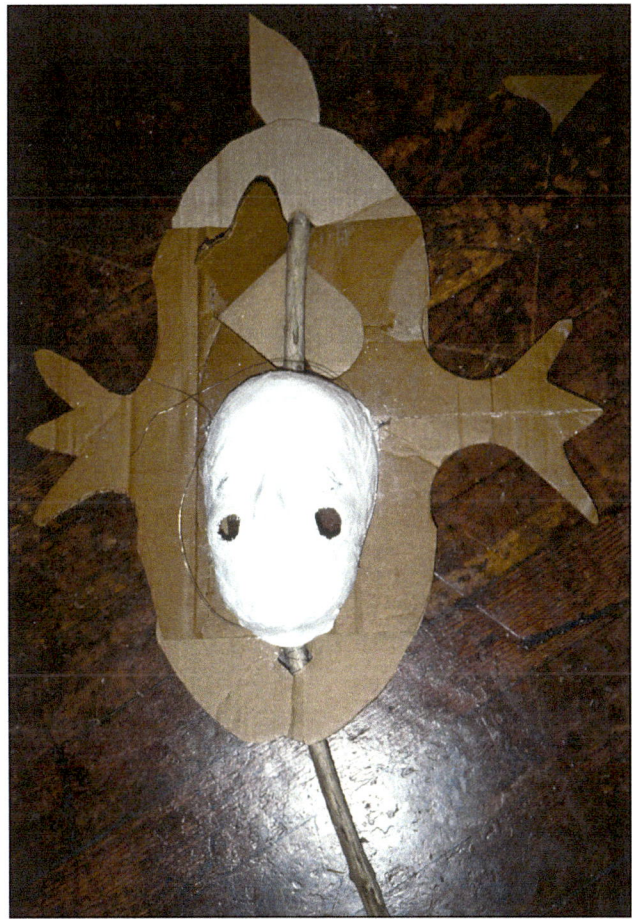

Anja: Forest Spirit

Painting and Adorning the Mask

Once the mask molds are sculpted to satisfaction and completely dry, it is time for students to prepare to paint and adorn their masks. If you do not have access to a wide variety of art materials, you can have students share in a supply potluck, each one bringing supplies to share, while you provide paints and tools. But if you can provide the art materials (with your fees adjusted accordingly), it is like inviting participants to partake of a big creative banquet. We typically bring a pickup truck loaded with organized bins of art materials. Use common sense when selecting materials. If you are teaching in jails or psychiatric facilities, be aware that some art supplies and tools, like sharp scissors, knives, and even raffia, may be contraband. You may want to bring low-temperature glue guns.

We usually first do a demonstration on painting and adorning the mask to prime both the readiness of the craftsperson and the appetite of the muse. We offer tips for using various media, but we are most interested in encouraging freedom and exploration with the materials. Then we invite students to set up their work spaces by covering the tables, getting paper towels and bowls of water for paintbrushes, setting out glue guns (on paper plates to protect the surrounding surfaces) ready for plugging in, and placing their masks ready and waiting to dance with the muse.

We give students the following basic pointers on painting and adorning:

- Apply gesso to the front and the back of the mask mold after it is completely dry to help protect it and seal the pores; however, this not necessary when working with acrylics. If using oil bars and oil pastels, markers, or inks directly on the mask mold, it would be a good idea to apply gesso to it first.

- Use the acrylic gel medium for collage, texturing, and glazing. Gels can be added to dirt, sand, pigments, herbs, spices, paint, or glitter for adhesive qualities. Gloss and matte acrylic gels dry clear.

- Use the magical but powerful regular temperature (hot) glue guns for adhering items (fabric, fur, feathers, beads, cardboard, etc.). Be cautious, as they can melt plastic or burn skin. If you prefer, use low-temperature glue guns.

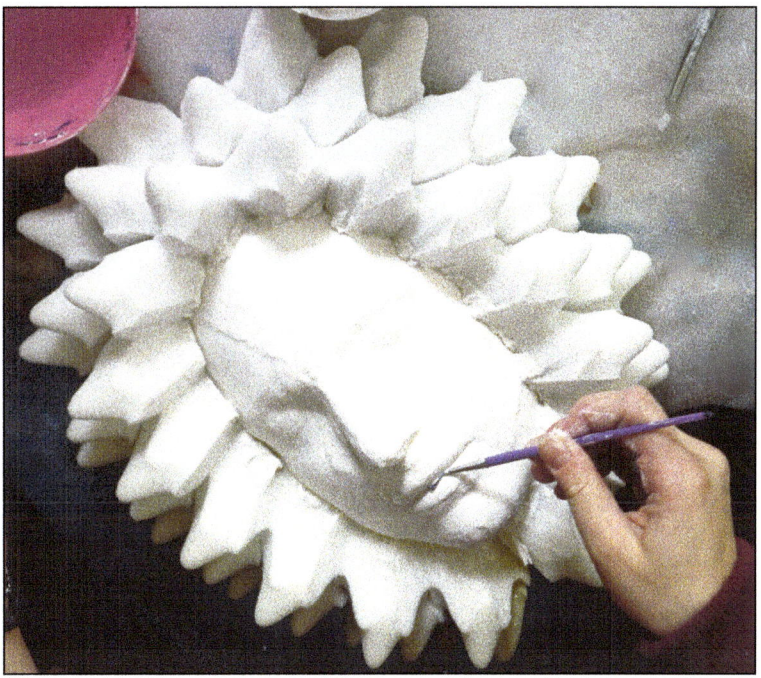

Preparing the mask with gesso

- If you like, start with chalk pastels, charcoal, graphite, color pencils, inks, pens, or markers on your mask mold. Some of these can be erased, wiped off, or painted over. Using fixative (outdoors) adds a seal. Acrylics can go on top of this layer.

- Use oil pastels on top of (not underneath) dry acrylic paint.

- Sprinkle glitter on wet paint or gel medium to change the mood of the painting.

- Leave things such as paint, acrylic gel medium, herbs, and glitter at the central location, so others don't have to go looking for them. Use paper plates for palettes to carry paint, acrylic gel medium, glitter, herbs, and beads.

- Mix the paint on the palette to explore color combinations (start with a small amount) or mix it directly on the mask.

- Gather supplies for your journey: Japanese rice paper for collage, balsa wood, wire, or cardboard for constructing, wigs, fabric, whatever your muse desires.

- Gather tools such as brushes (different sizes, bristle, sable), scissors, wire cutters, blade knife, needles, etc.

Then, prior to doing art, we take the students deeper on their inner explorations through guided imagery. When they emerge from the inner journey, they are ready to move straight to the creative one. We often prompt them, individually or as a group, with suggestions:

> You have just journeyed deeply and now linger at the portal between the subconscious and conscious realms. From this liminal state, play and create. Look at the art supplies and feast in the colors of paint. Rub the skins and stroke the gemstones. Smell the herbs and spices. Listen to the sounds of raffia rubbing on your fingertips or to the rustling of memory. Your soul is an honored guest at this banquet of colors, forms, textures. It accepts the invitation to feast on creativity. Give it permission to indulge its creative urges and whims. It may want to smear colored chalk with your fingers or seize different brushes to lather viscous paint or layer a thin sheath. It may want to rub in fur or fly with feathers or cloak itself in fine cloth or protect itself with amulets and medicine bundles. Sometimes your soul wants to dive deep. Sometimes it wants to laugh and play. It may want to speak through the sounds of your totem animal or the stories of the sage. Let your guides tell your story. Give yourself freedom to follow the impulses of your soul.

Media for Painting and Adorning the Masks

See "Selected Art Supply Resources" on page 76.

- We like to have acrylic paints of at least twenty-four colors. We like to include cadmium orange deep, hansa yellow light, yellow ochre, ultramarine blue, portrait pink, cadmium yellow medium, yellow green, cobalt blue, hot pink, burnt sienna, medium green, phthalo turquoise, napthol red light, alizarine crimson, phthalo blue, phthalo green, titanium white. We also include pearlescents: red pearl, ruby, royal gold, sapphire, silver, emerald, and turquoise pearl.

  Various sizes of paint brushes (sable, bristle, synthetic), metallic pigments, glitter, sequins, paper plates (palettes), palette sticks, acrylic gel media (matte, gloss, and pearlescent), modeling paste, lava gel, water bowl, sponges, paper towels

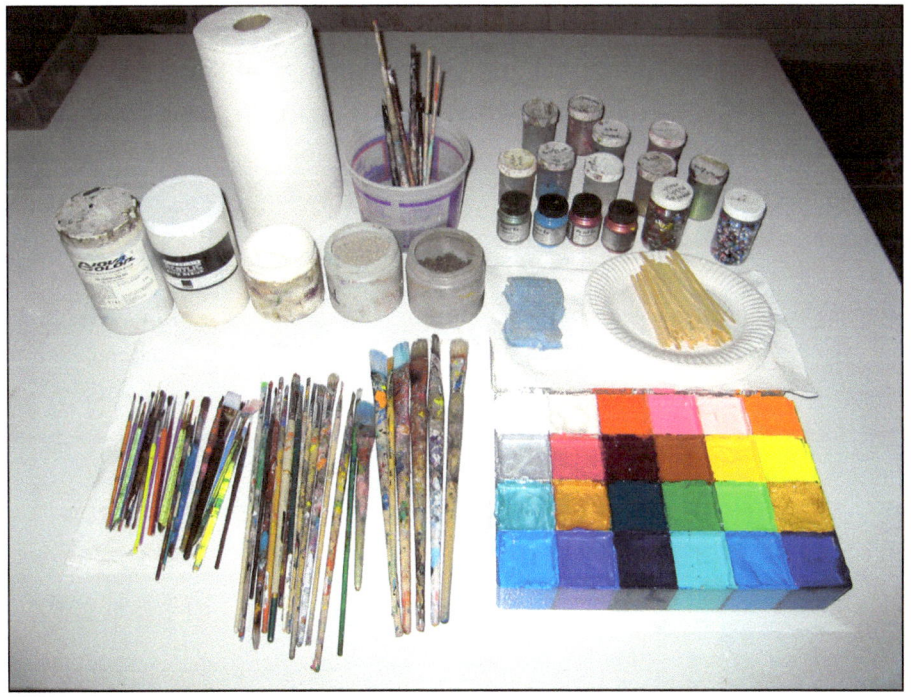

- Glitter, chalk, metallic pigments, powdered graphite, colored scenic sand, sequins, sand, dirt, fixative, paper towels

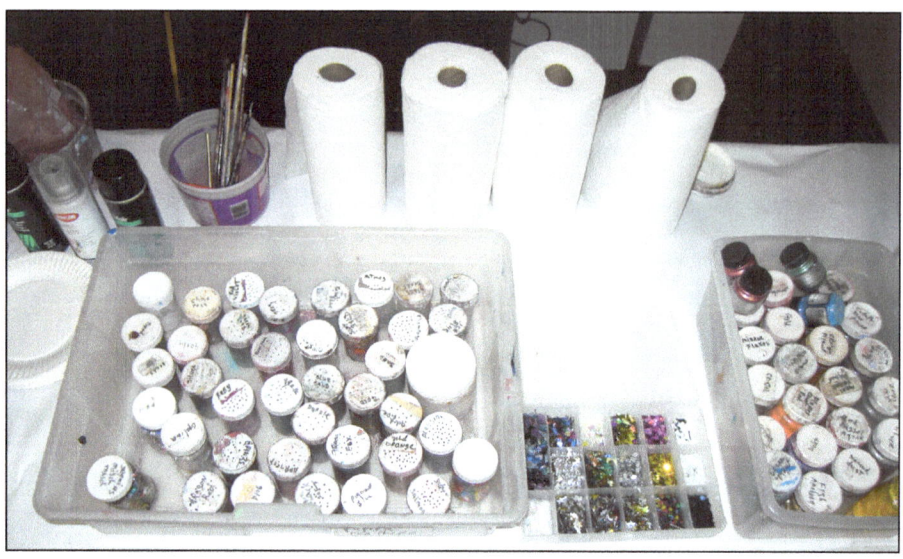

- Oil bars, baby oil, bones to draw with, water soluble artists' crayons, drawing and india inks, various markers, color pens, color pencils

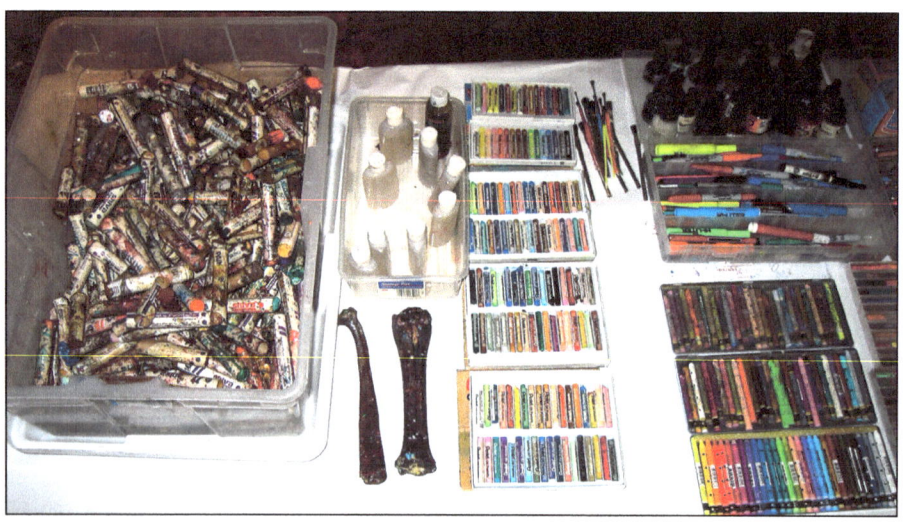

- Chalk and oil pastels, vine and compressed charcoal, conte crayons, graphite sticks, color pencils, rubber erasers, watercolor pencils, air-dry clay, workable matte fixatives (low-odor), gloss acrylic finishes, fimo, papier mache, sculptamold, elmer's glue, disposable gloves

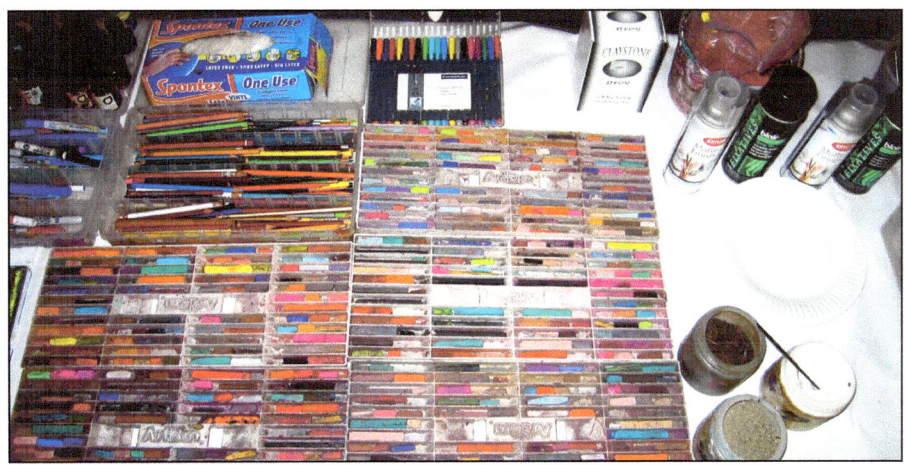

- Electric drill and bits, hair dryer, glue guns and glue sticks (we like to provide one glue gun per two students, so we bring many extension cords), scissors, scissors' sharpener, pencil sharpener, wire cutters, pliers, awls, screwdriver, hammer, industrial stapler and staples, clay tools, brayers, snap-off blade knives, x-acto knives, saw for wood, saw for metal, large metal ruler, jewelry and bent-nosed tweezers, framing wire (for mounting masks), copper, aluminum, and brass wire, fishing line, elastic, velcro, masking tape, wire scouring pad, sandpaper, various sizes of needles and threads, nails and screws, push pins, adaptor, matches

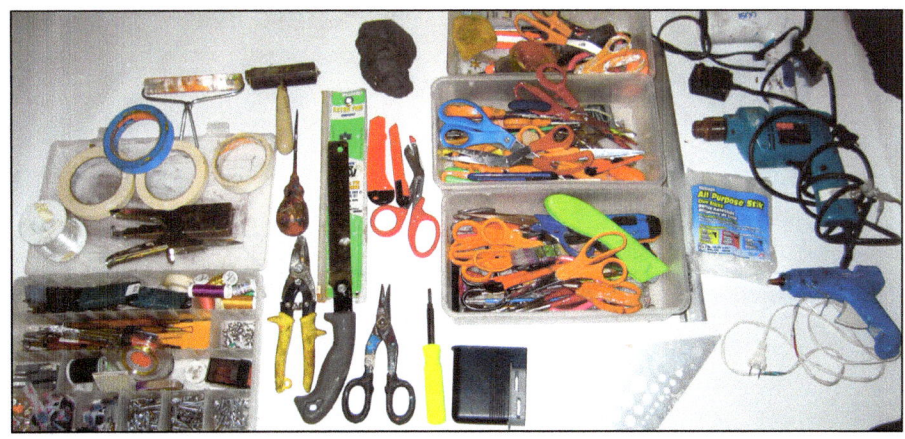

Other things we include are:

- Magazines and special papers (e.g., Japanese rice paper, Chinese joss papers, gold leaf, silver leaf, handmade paper) for collage

  Cardboard, canvas panels, canvas

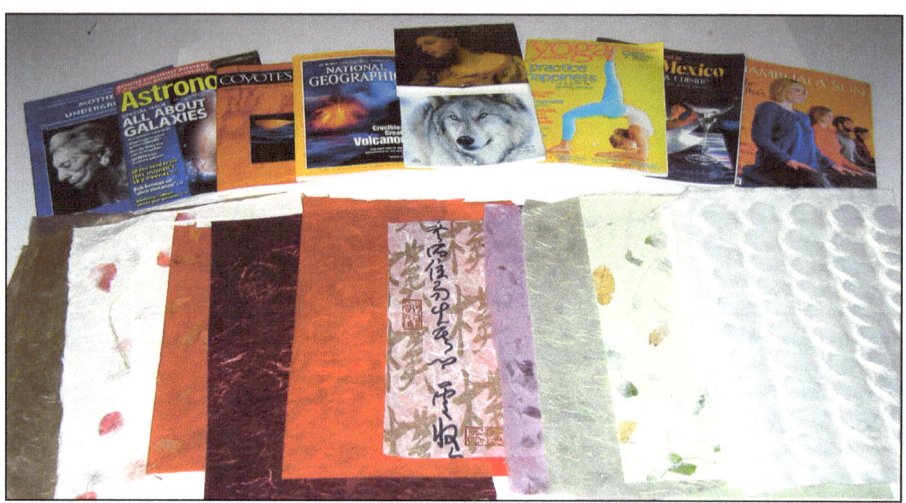

- Furs, rabbit skins, leather, vertebrae, leg and jaw bones, ram horns, horse manes and tails, camel hair, yak fur, deer antlers, snake skins

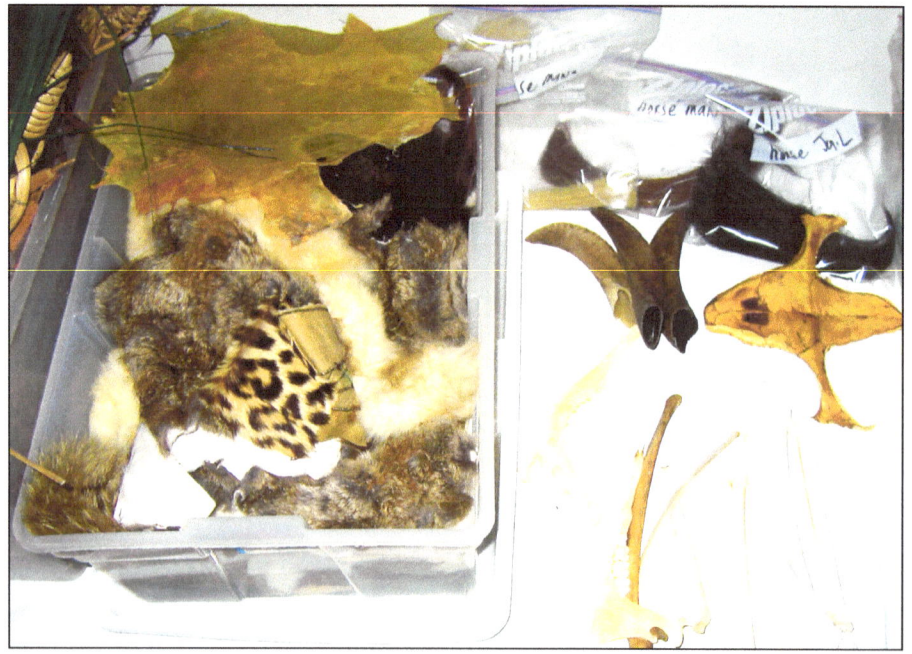

- Sisal, raffia, yarn, string, synthetic sinew, jute, hemp, and cotton twine

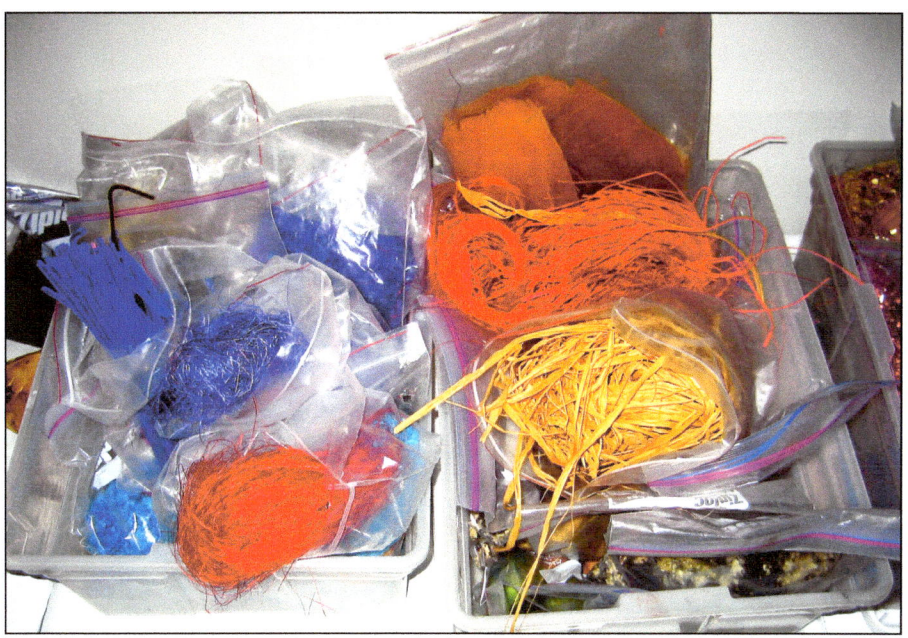

- Wrapping papers, masks, feathers, copper, brass, and aluminum tooling foil

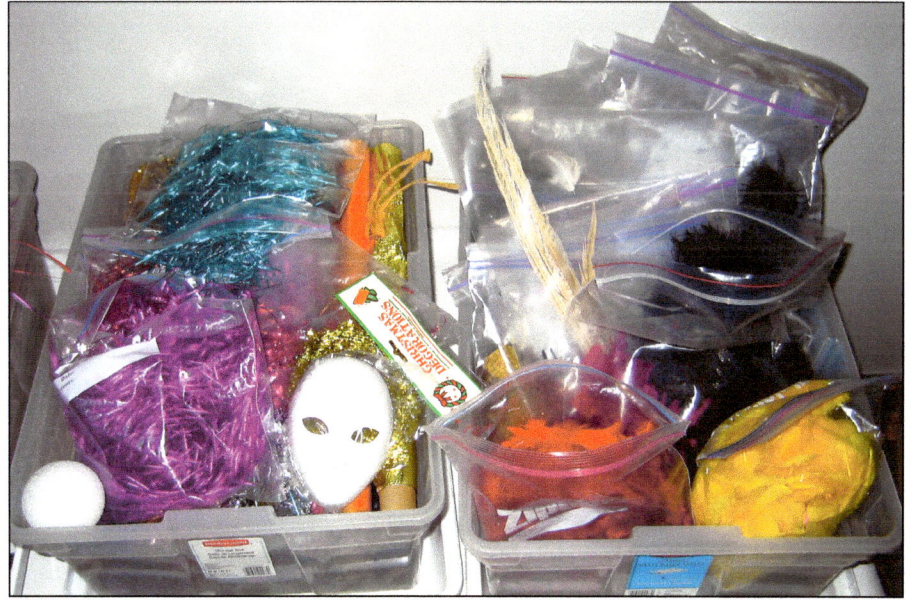

- Containers, wooden hinged and paper boxes and containers, wigs and hair

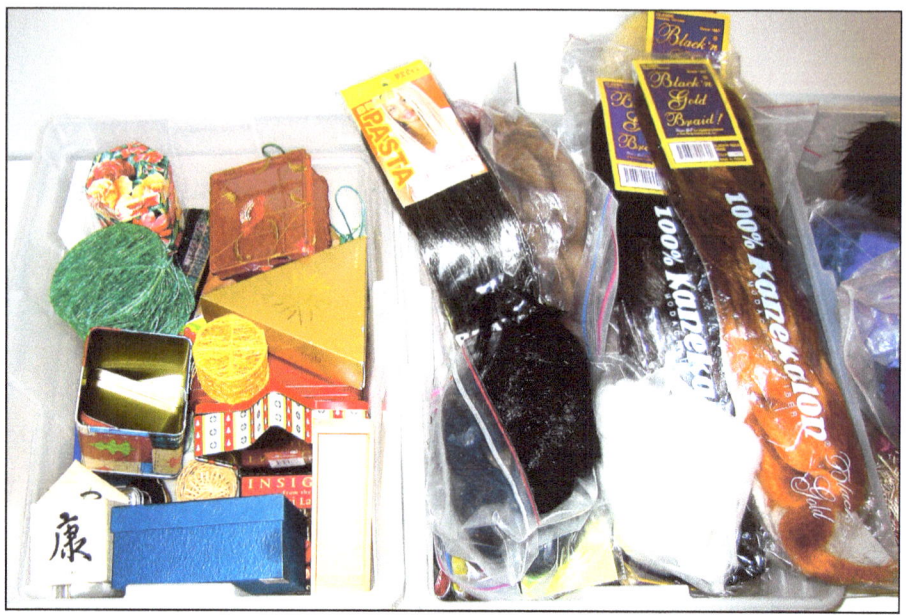

- Fabric (cheesecloth, burlap, cotton, canvas, silk, yarn)

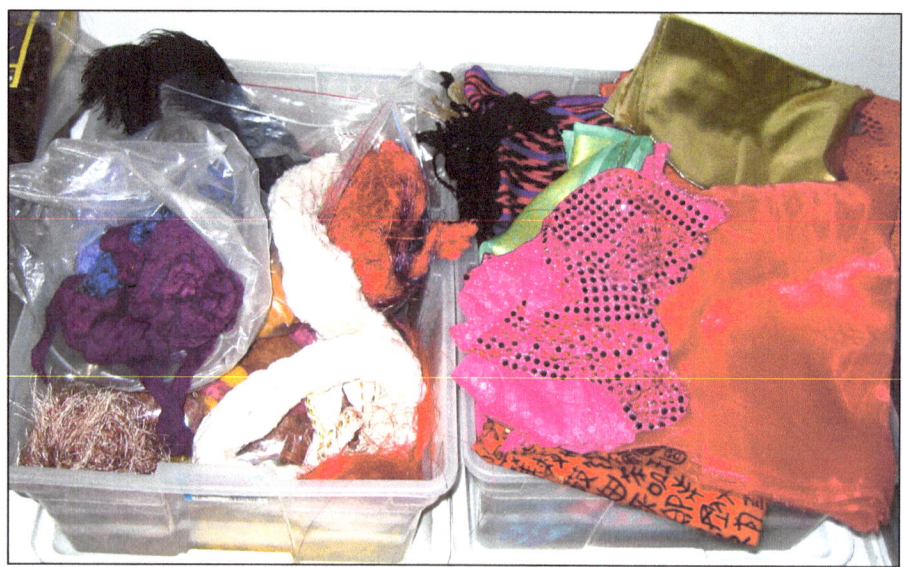

-

- Fabric, rope, styrofoam, metals, balsa wood, 14-gauge and 16-gauge sculpture wire, odds-and-ends, found and recycled objects

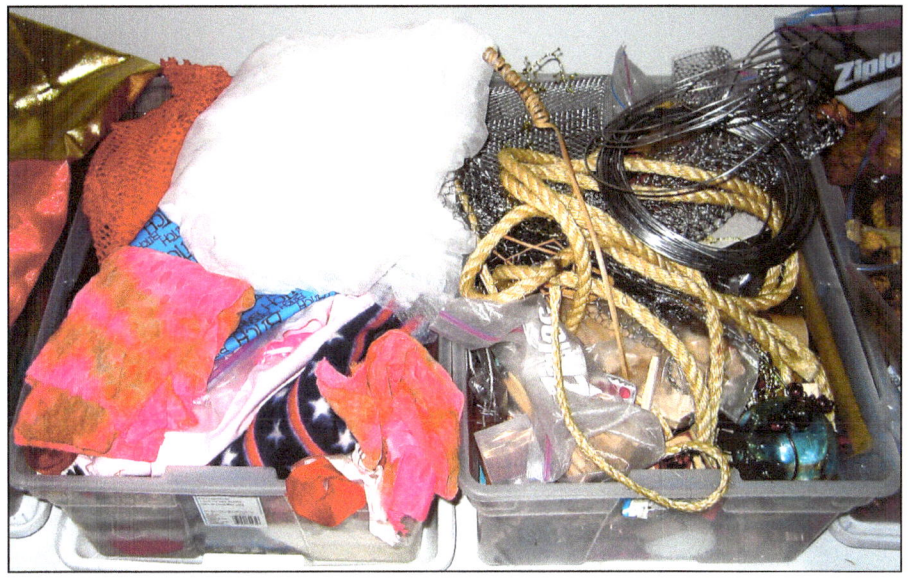

- Natural materials (e.g., baskets, handmade paper, sticks, branches, bamboo torch, etc.)

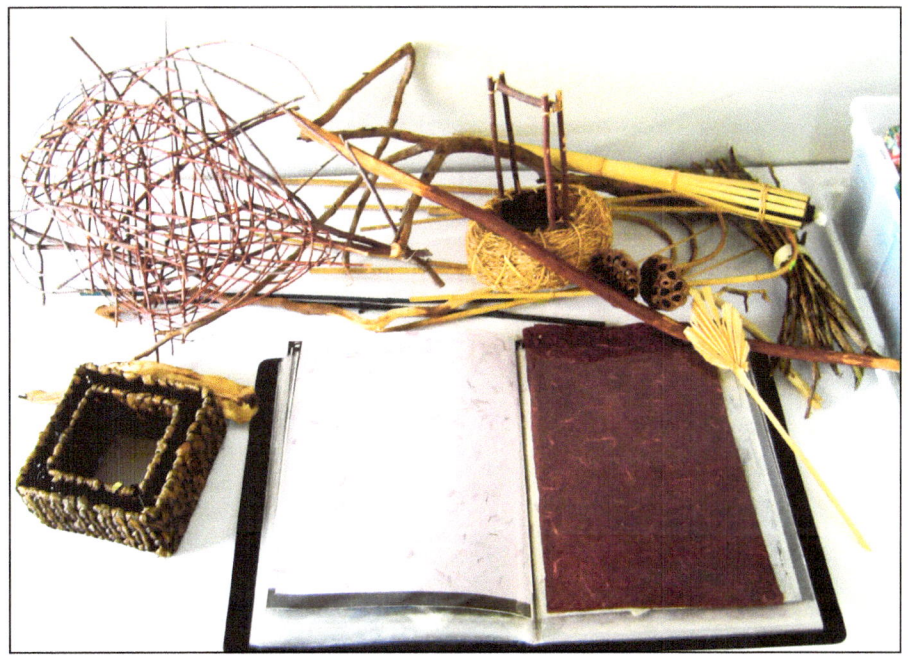

- Natural materials from floral supply stores (e.g., pods, dried flowers and leaves, bark, fungus, palm fronds, lotus leaves, moss)

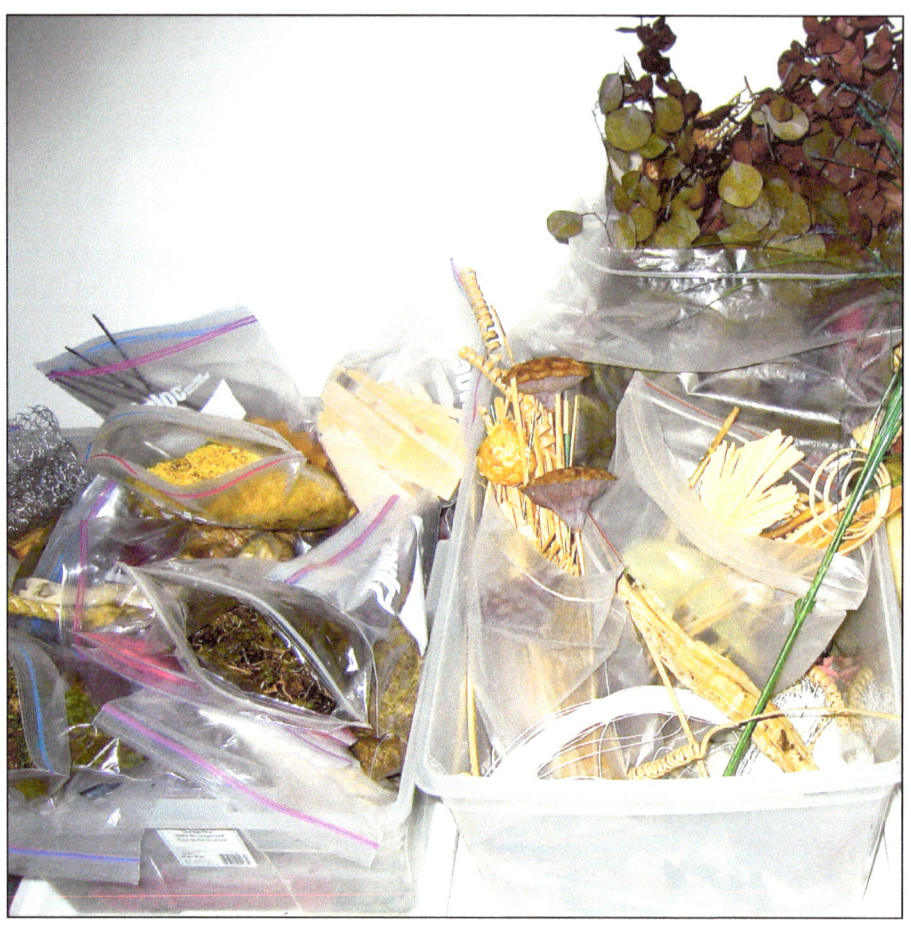

- Charms, gemstones, crystals, fossils, shells, ornaments, costume jewelry, scrabble letters, Native American, African, Asian, and European beads and ornaments, spiritual medallions and icons, totem animal charms, dentalium, foreign coins and bills, animal figurines, fish vertebrae, marbles, glass globs, mosaic squares, acrylic gems, bells, rune stones, fortune cookie fortunes, I Ching sticks, balloons, toys, copper enameling shapes, pendants, various sequins, etc.

Herbs (Chinese and western); see *Faces of Your Soul* pp. 205-210, for a list of herbs

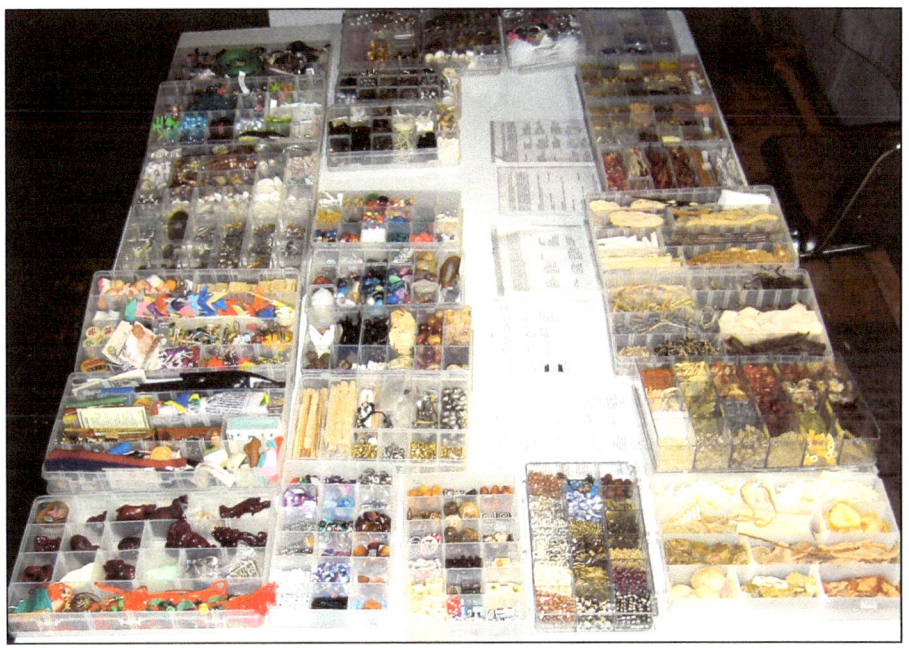

Sharing the Process

Talking about art is communication. The sharing of art is as powerful for the listeners as for the person sharing. Any comments by others should be supportive and appreciative. The sharing is not about interpreting or explaining; it is another level of transformation. We often invite a student to share from or as the creation rather than about it.

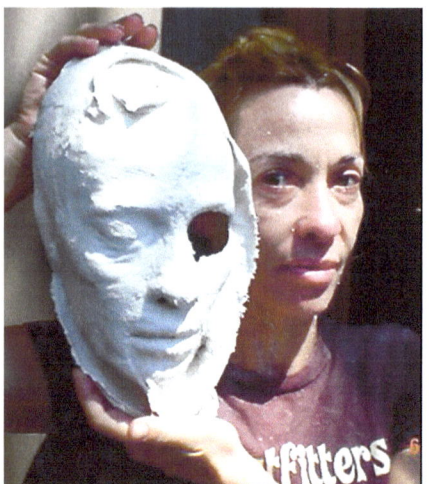 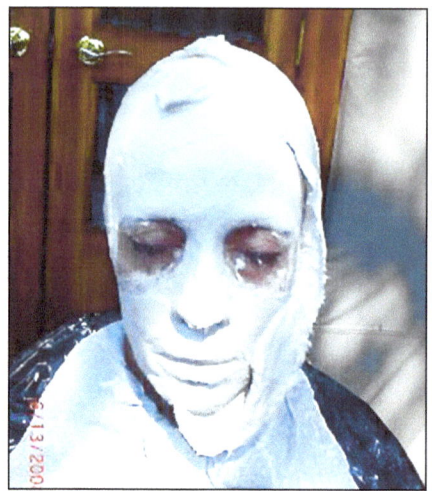

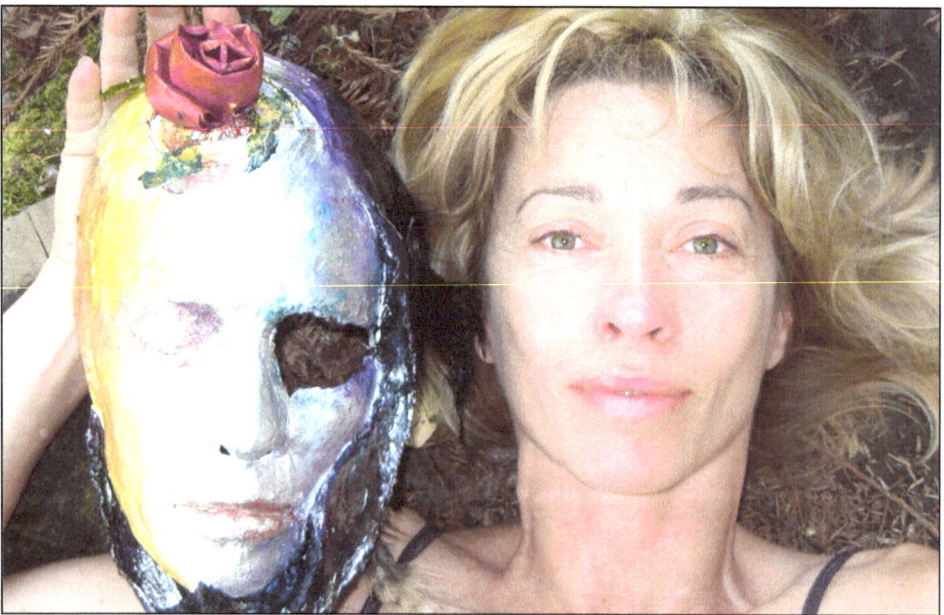

Laura: Sharing her gift

After the art process you may have the students sit before their pieces, look at them, understand them more deeply, then take five minutes to do automatic writing from their discoveries. Afterward, sharing their discoveries with the group manifests their transformation in communal reality.

Another option is to guide the students as a group back into subconscious realms to do ceremony with their masks and inner guides. When they emerge to awareness in the group, they share from this liminal place.

Sometimes students prefer to share in ways other than speaking. One student may put her ancestral mask before her face and move in the tasks and rituals of the ancestor. Another may growl and pounce as his tiger mask-totem. Another may sing her midwife-mask's song. Another may spontaneously choreograph his mask's dancing Chi Kung. We suggest you encourage the same freedom in sharing as in art-making. It is all a journey of discovery.

It is important for participants to feel safe in the sharing. Often students want to share their images and stories with others and reflect this by signing the photo permission form. But sometimes they want to keep their stories private, and when they indicate this, their desire for confidentiality should be honored. In such cases, no discussion of their sharing should go beyond the room. And the sharing of stories and images from classes should always be done with respect for the sanctity of the process.

Documentation

Sometime during class make sure the participants have signed the photo permission/mailing list if they agree. Then photograph the process. Documentation is a practical aid for advertising and teaching. After the workshop email the photos with a contact emailing list to the participants; they may want to keep in touch and continue their process.

Photos are a priceless way to preserve the process and communicate about it with others. You can use the photos in a slide presentation to inspire others in future maskmaking classes or in sharing the work with a wider community. Our students' photos and stories have been shared with many through their presence in our two books (Faces of Your Soul and Chi and Creativity) and Kaleo's album of over 1,000 student photos on Flickr.com: www.flickr.com/

photos/kaleoching. This 'ohana (family) expands by listing students' websites/ blogs or contact information with their photos. Your documentation is a way for you and others to share their journeys and stories and to infuse many, many others with awe and inspiration for creative process, personal growth, and self-empowerment.

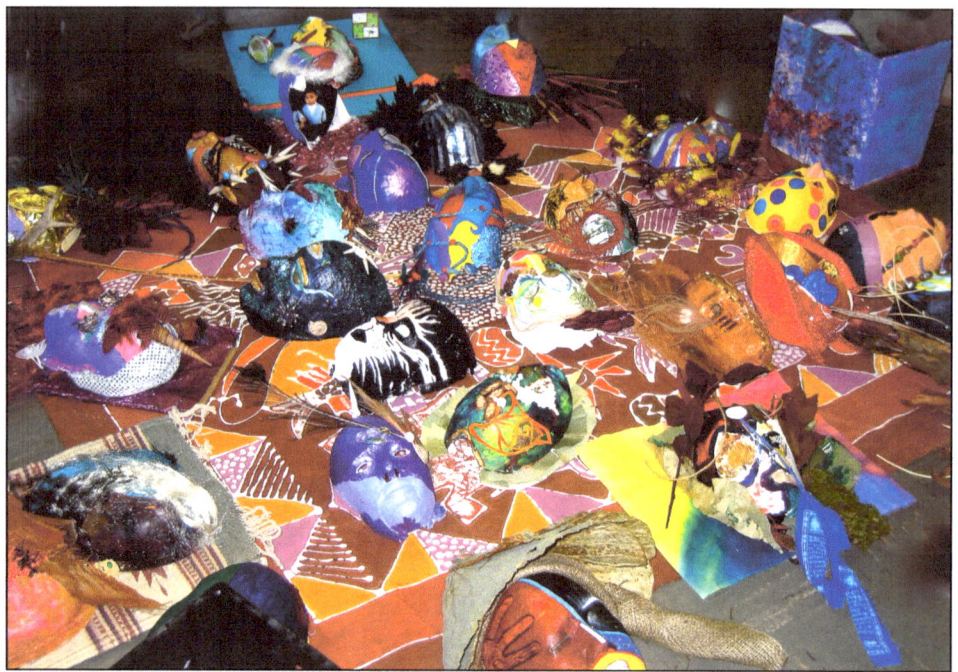

Altar of masks: SF State University Holistic Health class (with Ruth Cox, Kaleo, and Elise)

Your Legacy

Your workshop is over. The students' radiant faces and profound masks linger in the images of your camera and their stories echo in your heart. Your shared transformational journey continues. You continue to touch each other in memory and in an ongoing promise—that epiphany and wonder and creative discovery are real and have the power to change lives positively, with a rippling effect that radiates outward in all directions.

The techniques you employed you share in common with others, but you in your role of teacher and guide are unique. You are continuing and deepening something that started as a seed in you long ago, that sprouted, emerged, blossomed, and now shares seeds with others. Yours is a legacy of the joy of creative discovery, and you bring your own personal intention, style, gifts, and vision to the journey.

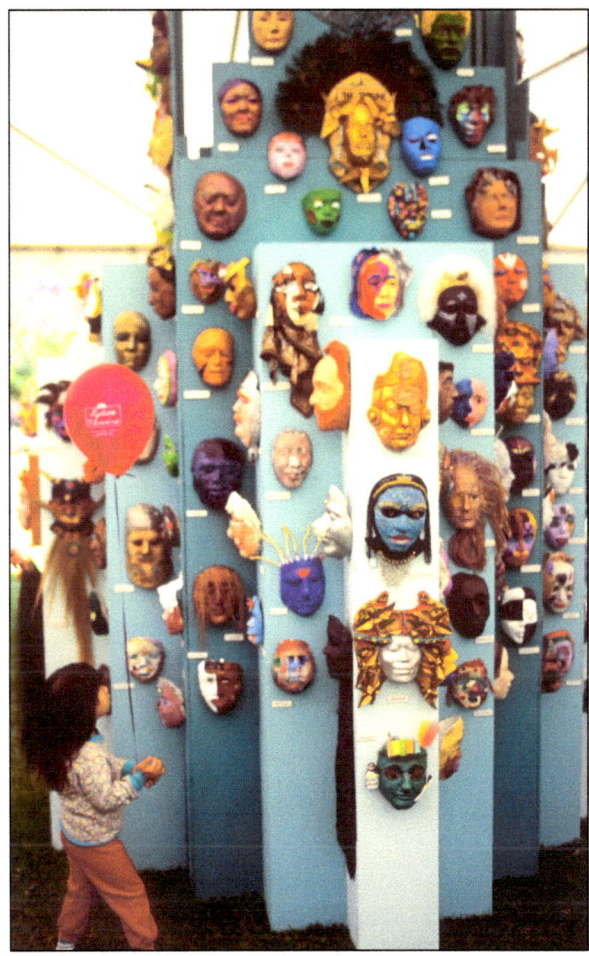

**Oakland Festival at the Lake 1,000 Faces Community Maskmaking Project
(Sas Colby, Bre Carrington, Susan Kaplan, facilitators)**

Journaling

Describe your personal legacy. What are you creating in and leaving for the world? How are you as teacher and guide growing spiritually and personally through the process? What is your unique contribution? How is it evolving? How is the world changing into a more hopeful place through who you are and what you share? When you have passed to the world of ancestors, how will you be remembered? What gifts of presence and spirit will you leave behind.

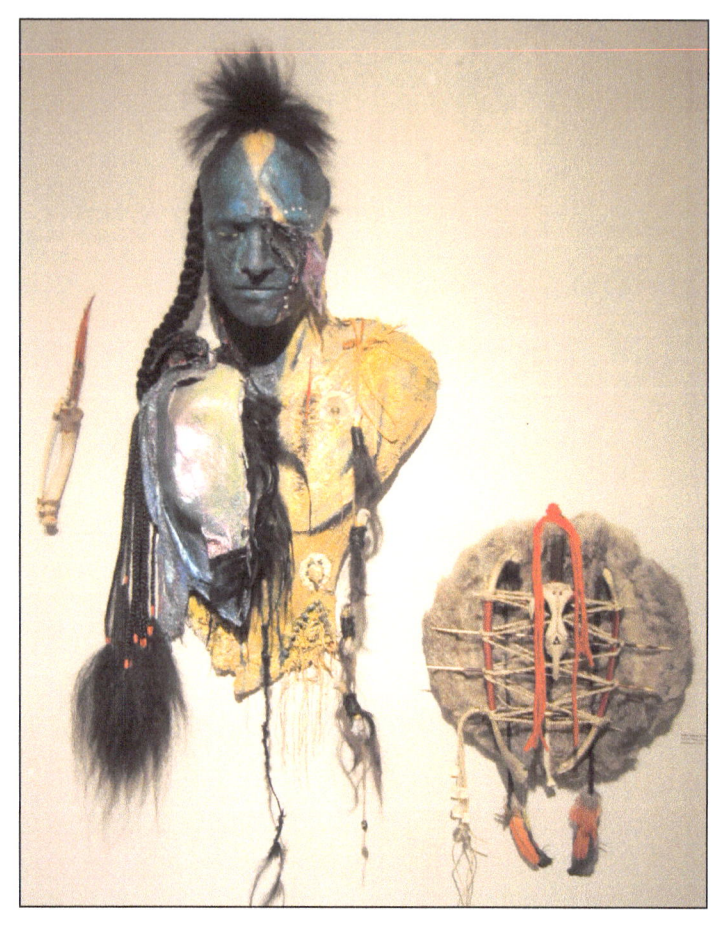

Warrior-Sage

Mixed Media Plaster Gauze Torso Mask by Kaleo Ching
Poem by Elise Dirlam Ching

Align your axis with the heavens when you walk.
Keep your grace down the long corridor of forgotten questions.
Expect no mercy.
Keep company with death,
who appears swiftly to some, hesitantly to others,
or unexpectedly as a lighthouse on the lost sea.
Keep your promises to your ancestors, your teachers, yourself,
those who seek you, the big heart of the universe.
Build your honor downward—
a funnel cloud spinning from the heavens.

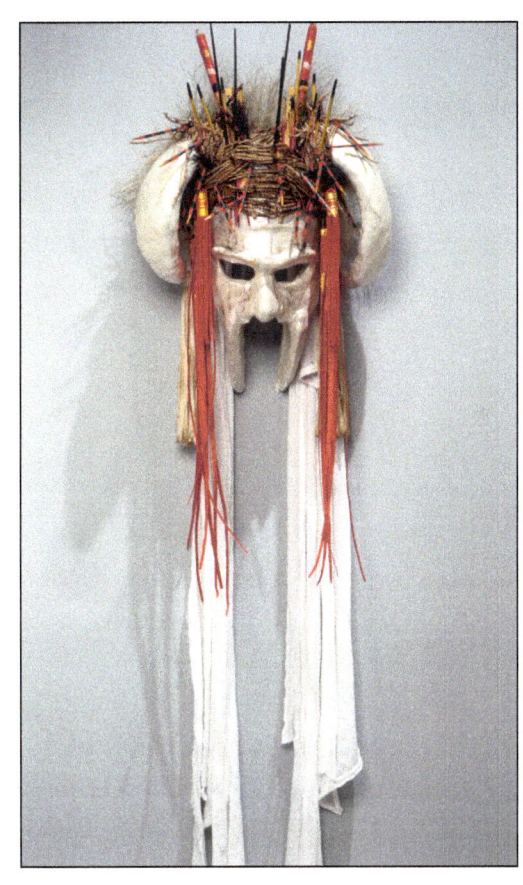

Charon

Mixed Media Plaster Gauze Mask by Kaleo Ching
Poem by Elise Dirlam Ching

Oar churning swiftly
against black water
ferryman of souls
grief and fear
beat black wings
about your shoulders
face like marble
feet feeling the stern
bow pointing toward the light
oar dipping silently
into black water

Sample Flyer: Your Warrior-Healer Mask

For more information on creating your own flyer, see "Flyer" on page 27
Original flyer 8½ by 11 inches

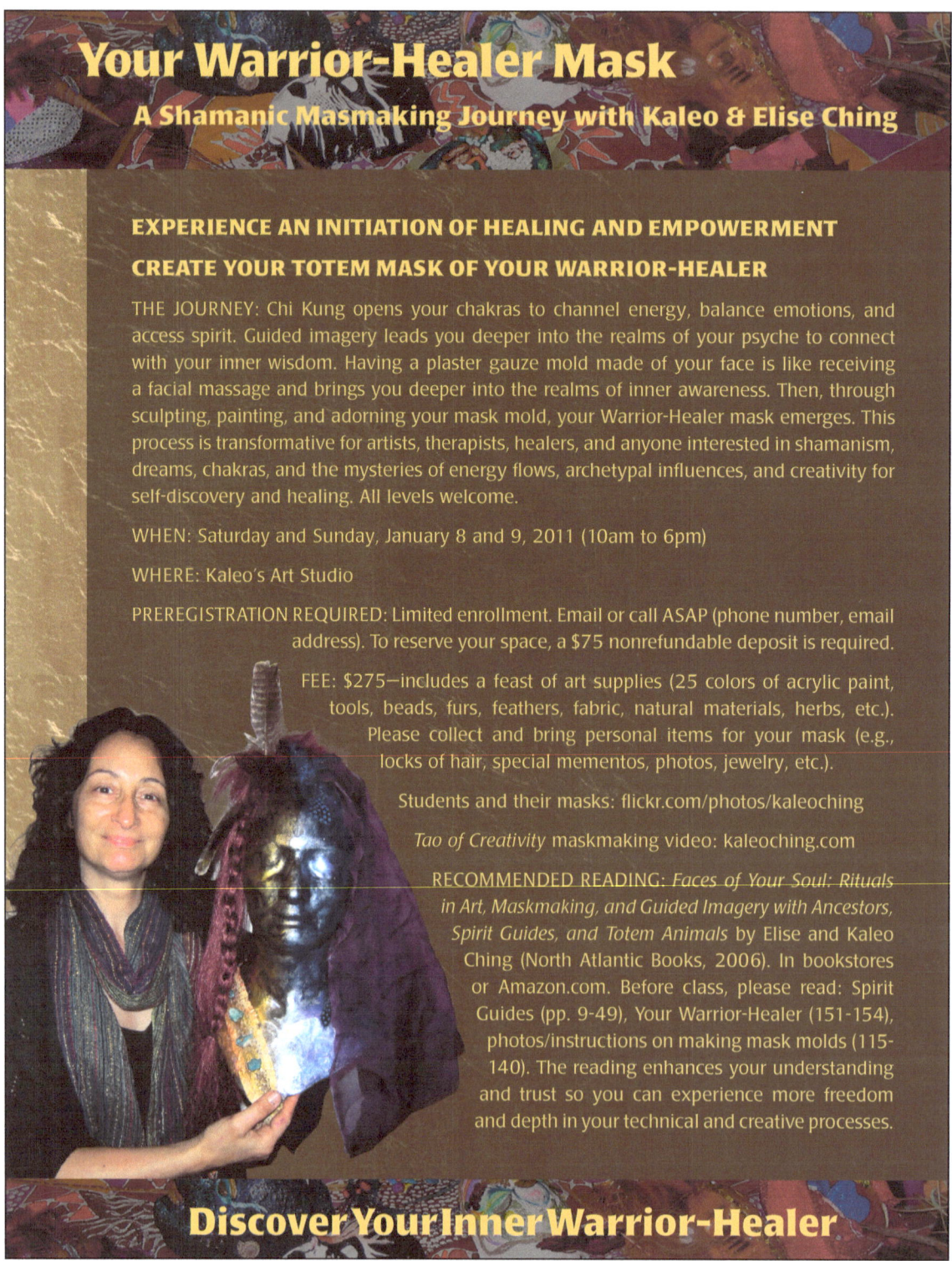

Your Warrior-Healer Mask
A Shamanic Masmaking Journey with Kaleo & Elise Ching

EXPERIENCE AN INITIATION OF HEALING AND EMPOWERMENT

CREATE YOUR TOTEM MASK OF YOUR WARRIOR-HEALER

THE JOURNEY: Chi Kung opens your chakras to channel energy, balance emotions, and access spirit. Guided imagery leads you deeper into the realms of your psyche to connect with your inner wisdom. Having a plaster gauze mold made of your face is like receiving a facial massage and brings you deeper into the realms of inner awareness. Then, through sculpting, painting, and adorning your mask mold, your Warrior-Healer mask emerges. This process is transformative for artists, therapists, healers, and anyone interested in shamanism, dreams, chakras, and the mysteries of energy flows, archetypal influences, and creativity for self-discovery and healing. All levels welcome.

WHEN: Saturday and Sunday, January 8 and 9, 2011 (10am to 6pm)

WHERE: Kaleo's Art Studio

PREREGISTRATION REQUIRED: Limited enrollment. Email or call ASAP (phone number, email address). To reserve your space, a $75 nonrefundable deposit is required.

FEE: $275—includes a feast of art supplies (25 colors of acrylic paint, tools, beads, furs, feathers, fabric, natural materials, herbs, etc.). Please collect and bring personal items for your mask (e.g., locks of hair, special mementos, photos, jewelry, etc.).

Students and their masks: flickr.com/photos/kaleoching

Tao of Creativity maskmaking video: kaleoching.com

RECOMMENDED READING: *Faces of Your Soul: Rituals in Art, Maskmaking, and Guided Imagery with Ancestors, Spirit Guides, and Totem Animals* by Elise and Kaleo Ching (North Atlantic Books, 2006). In bookstores or Amazon.com. Before class, please read: Spirit Guides (pp. 9-49), Your Warrior-Healer (151-154), photos/instructions on making mask molds (115-140). The reading enhances your understanding and trust so you can experience more freedom and depth in your technical and creative processes.

Discover Your Inner Warrior-Healer

Sample Handout: Studio Considerations

(For more information on creating your own Studio Considerations handout, see "Studio Considerations" on page 28.)

In sharing this studio, please be considerate. Respect each other's physical and subconsious space. Please keep conversation to a minimum.

Preparation

- Dress comfortably and safely for making art.

- Help bring in and set up supplies.

- Help set up the studio (arrange tables and chairs, cover tables and floor).

- Assist in setting up mask mold making workstations (per pair): gauze, scissors, tape, plastic bag, plastic wrap, two brushes, plastic water bowl, petroleum jelly, oil-based lotion, paper towels.

Studio Use and Safety

- *Caution when using blade knives.* Use cardboard to protect the tables and floor. Use the large metal ruler to cut with blade knives. Sheathe knives. Keep sharp tools off the floor.

- *Caution with electric drill.* Seek help from the teacher and wear safety glasses.

- *Use toxic materials outside* (e.g., fixative).

- *Protect your feet. Wear shoes.*

- *No children, pets, or visitors* during class.

- *Protect the plumbing.* Empty plaster of paris and dirty water in the trash, not the sink.

- *Protect brushes.* Keep them in your water containers when not in use.

- Leave things such as paint, acrylic gel medium, herbs, and glitter at the central location so others know where to find them. Use paper plates for palettes to carry paint, acrylic gel medium, glitter, herbs, and beads back to your work table.

- Gather supplies for your creative journey: Japanese rice paper for collage, balsa wood, wire, or cardboard for constructing, wigs, fabric, whatever your muse desires.

- Gather tools such as brushes (different sizes, bristle, sable), scissors, wire cutters, blade knife, needles, etc.

Studio Clean-up

- Keep the supplies protected in their bags. Fold the fabric pieces so others can use them.

- Return supplies to their appropriate bins and containers.

- One person please collect and wash all paint brushes thoroughly with soap and water.

- One person please collect and clean bowls. Pour dirty water into the trash, not the sink.

- Two people please collect and clean tools (scissors, rulers, glue guns, extension cords, etc.).

- Everyone cleans his/her area and sponges the table.

- Everyone helps clean and fold tarps, sweep floor, carry out the supplies.

Sample: Photo Permission/Mailing List

(For more information on creating your own Photo Permission/Mailing List, see "Photo Permission/Mailing List" on page 28.)

Teacher:_____Date:_____

Class:_____Location: _____

I agree that [teacher's name here] may use my photos for written/educational materials or PR. I agree that he/she may tell my story from a teacher's perspective.

1. Name (Print):_____Email:_____

Address:_____Phone:_____

Signature:_____Date:_____

2. Name (Print):_____Email:_____

Address:_____Phone:_____

Signature:_____Date:_____

3. Name (Print):_____Email:_____

Address:_____Phone:_____

Signature:_____Date:_____

4. Name (Print):_____Email:_____

Address:_____Phone:_____

Signature:_____Date:_____

5. Name (Print):_____Email:_____

Address:_____Phone:_____

Signature:_____Date:_____

6. Name (Print):_____Email:_____

Address:_____Phone:_____

Signature:_____Date:_____

7. Name (Print):_____Email:_____

Address:_____Phone:_____

Signature:_____Date:_____

Selected Art Supply Resources

(For more information on art supplies, see "Media for Painting and Adorning the Masks" on page 57.)

Artstuf (large quantities of plaster gauze): www.artstuf.com

Blick: www.dickblick.com

Joann Fabrics: www.joann.com

Michael's Art Supplies: www.michaels.com

Nova Color (paints): www.novacolor.com

Utrecht: www.UtrechtArt.com

White Fox Furs, Feathers (Jay and Natalie): whitefoxfur@juno.com

Florists' equipment and supply stores, Asian herbal stores, flea markets, bead stores, rock stores, hardware stores.

The Authors

Kaleo Ching, M.A. Art, CAMT, CCHT, and **Elise Dirlam Ching**, RN, M.A., CAMT, CCHT, teach their holistic process integrating Chi Kung, guided imagery, and transformative art and maskmaking as a journey to inner wisdom and discovery of the sacred within. They teach at John F. Kennedy University, Wisdom University, and CIIS Public Programs and workshops in the Bay Area and beyond.

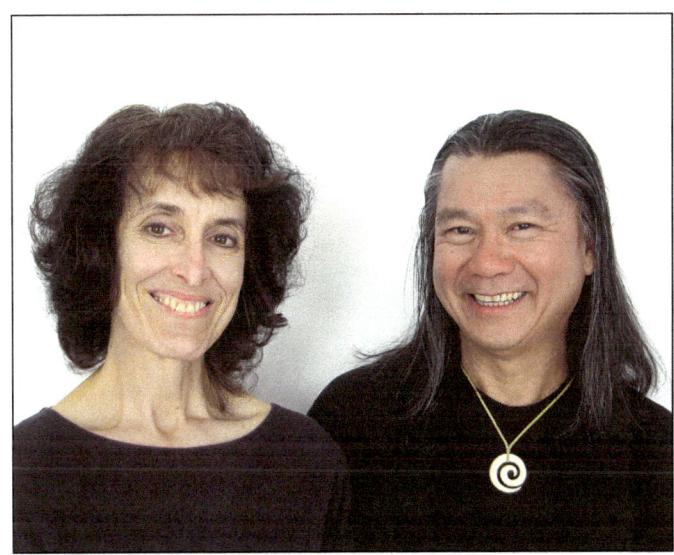

Kaleo also teaches Chi Kung and bodywork classes at the Acupressure Institute and has a private bodywork and hypnotherapy practice in Walnut Creek, California.

They coauthored *Faces of Your Soul: Rituals in Art, Maskmaking and Guided Imagery with Ancestors, Spirit Guides, and Totem Animals*, published by North Atlantic Books, 2006, and *Chi and Creativity: Vital Energy and Your Inner Artist*, published by Blue Snake Books, 2007. They are currently writing *The Pilgrimage: Your Personal Explorations of Dying and Rebirth*.

Visit www.kaleoching.com

www.ingramcontent.com/pod-product-compliance
Lightning Source LLC
Chambersburg PA
CBHW051022180526
45172CB00002B/441